KT-217-153

Good Food Made Simple

BRITISH

Good Food Made Simple

BRITISH

Over 140 delicious recipes, 500 colour photographs, step-by-step images and nutritional information

This edition published by Parragon Books Ltd in 2014
LOVE FOOD is an imprint of Parragon Books Ltd

Parragon Books Ltd
Chartist House
15–17 Trim Street
Bath BA1 1HA, UK
www.parragon.com/lovefood

ISBN: 978-1-4723-5699-4

Printed in China

Additional design by Geoff Borin
New photography by Mike Cooper
New home economy by Lincoln Jefferson
New recipes by Teresa Goldfinch and Angela Drake
Introduction and notes by Angela Drake
Nutritional analysis by Fiona Hunter

Notes for the Reader
This book uses both metric and imperial measurements. Follow the same units of measurement throughout; do not mix metric and imperial. All spoon measurements are level: teaspoons are assumed to be 5 ml, and tablespoons are assumed to be 15 ml. Unless otherwise stated, milk is assumed to be full fat, eggs and individual vegetables are medium, and pepper is freshly ground black pepper. Unless otherwise stated, all root vegetables should be peeled prior to using.

Garnishes, decorations and serving suggestions are all optional and not necessarily included in the recipe ingredients or method. Any optional ingredients and seasoning to taste are not included in the nutritional analysis. The times given are an approximate guide only. Preparation times differ according to the techniques used by different people and the cooking times may also vary from those given. Optional ingredients, variations or serving suggestions have not been included in the time calculations.

Contents

British food – a world of flavours

Many of the traditional British recipes that we know and love today are steeped in history. Through the centuries, our cultural heritage, varying religions and the changeable climate of the British Isles have all had a major influence on the produce grown and imported into the country. All of these elements have helped to shape the recipes that have become known as the best of British cookery.

A brief history of British cuisine

As an island nation, Britain owes much of its food heritage to many other far-flung countries. England was ruled by the Romans for over 400 years and they introduced produce such as venison, geese and pheasant to this country. In Anglo-Saxon times, food was simple and basic with meat dishes and herb-flavoured stews being the order of the day until the Normans bought a vast array of produce from Europe, including fragrant spices such as saffron, nutmeg, pepper and cloves, as well as almonds and sugar.

Food for the wealthy during the Middle Ages was full of richly spiced sweet and savoury dishes, as well as puddings and baked goods. However, the rural poor had to make do with plain and simple fare based on vegetable broths and pottages served with rustic breads and honey-sweet mead. What we know as the traditional Sunday roast originated during these medieval times – Sunday was the only day of rest and spit-roasted oxen was eaten by the peasants after morning church services.

The traditional Sunday roast originated during medieval times when Sunday was the only day of rest.

During the 16th and 17th centuries, as explorers travelled around the globe, even more exotic and unusual produce became available. Much of the produce came from the newly discovered Americas, including potatoes, coffee and vanilla. By the early 19th century, Britain had colonized much of the world. Tea was imported from Asia and spiced sauces and condiments were popular, as they still are today – just think of tomato ketchup and Worcestershire sauce! However, there was still a huge difference between the luxurious and very opulent diets of the rich and the woefully meagre, cheap food that much of the population survived on.

This all changed by the 20th century when two World Wars resulted in imported goods becoming scarce. Meat, dairy produce and sugar were strictly rationed for everyone – rich or poor. The national diet during this time was based mainly on home-grown vegetables and bread.

In the decades following World War II, technological advances in food processing, refrigeration and freezing meant that many seasonal goods could be available all year round and at affordable prices. Mass-produced convenience food became plentiful and interest in home cooking began to decline.

In recent years there has been a renewed interest in our culinary history. Local growers are producing quality, seasonal produce to sell at farmers' markets and delis. Many of our tastiest, classic British recipes, from pies and puddings to cakes and breads, are enjoying a well-deserved revival and many have been re-invented with modern twists.

Round the regions

Wherever you travel in Great Britain, you'll find a wealth of wonderful home-grown produce and traditional recipes. Each region, county, town or small village may have its own speciality, often linked to local produce or a specific religious or seasonal event. Many have become national favourites that are famous worldwide, such as Yorkshire Puddings and Cornish Pasties.

The Scottish highland heathers attract bees that produce some sublime honey.

Scotland

Scotland is home to some of the finest game, meat, fish, fruit and vegetables in Britain. Venison, beef and salmon are full of natural flavour and are perfect for special occasions. Smoked fish, such as salmon and Arbroath smokies (a type of smoked haddock), are widely produced around the rugged coastline.

The long, light and cool summer days are ideal for growing the most delicious raspberries. The highland heathers attract bees that produce some sublime honey.

Traditional Scottish recipes are fairly simple but nourishing and wholesome. Porridge, Game Pie, Scotch Broth and Shortbread are just a few favourites that you may be familiar with.

Northern Ireland

A land of plentiful rainfall that keeps the pastures green and lush, Northern Ireland has a natural larder full of top class pork, beef, traditional cured bacon and dairy produce.

Potatoes have always been a staple Irish food and are the essential ingredient for some wonderfully filling stews, soups and side dishes, such as Colcannon. Simple rustic breads and bakes are classic favourites of Northern Ireland, such as Soda Bread or Potato Cakes.

The clear rivers and lakes provide a bountiful supply of fish, while shellfish, such as oysters and mussels are plentiful around the coast.

Wales

Farming has always been a part of Welsh life and the country is particularly well known for its delicious lamb along with its national vegetable – the leek.

However, dairy cattle also play a part in Welsh food heritage providing milk for salty butter and wonderful cheeses, such as Caerphilly or goat's cheese.

Caerphilly cheese can be used on traditional Welsh Rarebit.

Fruit cakes and breads have always been traditional high tea classics, along with stacks of pancakes or scones cooked on a hot griddle or on a baking stone on an open fire.

England

Just like the other countries that are part of Great Britain, England has a rich heritage of farming.

The cool damp climate ensures that there is a plentiful supply of home-grown produce, from beef, lamb and pork to seasonal vegetables. There is also an abundance of soft summer fruit, such as strawberries, plums and blackberries, as well as a whole variety of apples, such as Granny Smith or Cox's Pippin.

Certain regions of England are famous for their cheeses, such as Wensleydale, Stilton, Double Gloucester and, of course, the world famous Cheddar.

The many rivers running through the country are full of freshwater fish, such as trout and salmon, and the endless coastline is home to an abundance of seafood, from mackerel, monkfish and red mullet to crab, cockles and mussels. The many cities, towns, villages and counties of England all have their own regional specialities that are either made from locally grown produce or are in some way influenced by the social history of the area. The Cornish Pasty has its roots in the mining history of Cornwall, where workers would take the pasties down the mines with them for lunch. The pie's expensive meat would be protected by the hard crust of the pastry.

Some recipes are named after the places where they originated, such as Yorkshire Puddings, Melton Mowbray Pork Pies, Cheddar Cheese or Sussex Pond Pudding. Other recipes are inextricably linked to a certain area of the country, such as Lancashire Hot Pot from the North or Scones with Jam and Clotted Cream, a quintessential teatime treat from Devon and Cornwall.

Eating seasonally

It probably goes without saying that locally grown seasonal produce will have the finest and freshest flavour. Although nowadays we can buy just about anything all year round and supermarkets are full of exotic produce from all over the world, there are some British delicacies that are only at their best at certain times of the year. Here's a guide to what to look out for and when.

You can buy locally grown produce from a range of sources, such as local shops, markets, or door-to-door deliveries.

Pick of the crop

- Asparagus – the finest English asparagus will appear in early May and last for just a few weeks. Once it is picked, it rapidly loses its flavour so the fresher you can buy it, the better. Look for firm but tender stalks with closed tips. To best store asparagus before cooking, it is best to trim the ends and stand upright in a jar with 2.5 cm/1 inch of water in. Cover with a plastic bag and store in the refrigerator for up to 2 days.

  Snap off the woody ends of the asparagus before lightly steaming for 4–5 minutes.

- Summer fruit – look out for tart fresh gooseberries in early summer that are just perfect for sweet pies, fools and preserves. Fresh English cherries are in abundance in June, whilst June and July are the best months for sun-ripened strawberries. If possible, pick your own fruit for the ultimate in flavour and quality.

  Scottish raspberries and loganberries will appear in mid-summer – they freeze beautifully so it's worth stocking up for the winter months. Sharp fresh red, white and black currants are also packed full of flavour and vitamins and will be in good supply during August.

- Autumn fruits and nuts – the 'Garden of England' county of Kent produces a huge variety of apples, pears and plums through the early autumn months. Look out for old-fashioned varieties in farmers' markets or farm shops. Apples and plums can be used in traditional cobblers, pies and crumbles to provide comfort food for the colder autumn months. Chestnuts, walnuts, Kent cobnuts and hazelnuts come into season through autumn. They keep well and are perfect for festive Christmas recipes.

- Potatoes – May sees the arrival of delicious Jersey Royal potatoes with their unique creamy flavour.

Make the most of their short season then enjoy other varieties of home grown new potatoes through the summer months. Main crop potatoes are available throughout the rest of the year – Desirée, King Edward and Maris Piper are three classic British varieties.

- Vegetables – in spring, enjoy fresh vegetables such as young baby carrots, turnips and green and broad beans. During the summer months, choose from the abundance of salad vegetables, runner beans, fresh peas, mangetout and corn on the cob.

Make the most of squashes, pumpkins, courgettes and marrows in early autumn and, after the first frosts of winter, vegetables such as cauliflowers, carrots, sprouts, parsnips, swede and cabbages will be at their best.

And don't forget rhubarb – yes, it really is a vegetable! Look out for light pink forced rhubarb in late winter and the chunkier stalks of outdoor varieties in the shops in April.

- Good game – From the 'glorious' 12th of August, the season for hunting wild, feathered game begins and runs through until February. Furred game, such as pheasant, wild duck or partridge, is available from early August through to April.

Many supermarkets now sell ready prepared, locally produced game or buy from a local game dealer.

High days & holidays

Like any other nation the Brits love a party or seasonal celebration. Throughout history, food has always played an important part in any festivity and there are many traditional British recipes that are cooked on these special days and occasions.

There are many celebration days with connections to food in Britain but nothing can beat Christmas for the range of sweet treats available!

- Burns Night is a Scottish festivity that celebrates the poet Robert Burns' birthday on January 25th. Haggis is the centrepiece of the supper, usually piped into the dining room by bagpipes. Neeps and Tatties (mashed turnips and potatoes) are the traditional accompaniments, along with generous helpings of traditional Scotch whisky to wash down the delicious food.
- Shrove Tuesday, also known as Pancake Day, is always the last Tuesday before the Christian festival of Lent, a time of fasting. Traditionally, pancakes were made to use up the rich butter, milk and eggs forbidden during fasting. For most families these days it's a fun time to enjoy making and eating delicious sweet and savoury pancakes. Traditional toppings include sugar and lemon, chopped banana and chocolate sauce, or chopped apple and cinnamon.
- Easter is an important spring Christian celebration. Chocolate eggs are given and received by adults and children alike.

Traditional recipes that are served over the Easter weekend include fish dishes, such as Fisherman's Pie or Poached Salmon, Hot Cross Buns on Good Friday, and Roast Lamb, Simnel Cake and Easter Biscuits on Easter Sunday.

- Halloween is celebrated on October 31st and has become a favourite seasonal festivity, especially with children who love to go trick or treating in fancy dress. Pumpkins are carved out to make ghostly lanterns and, although there are no specific traditional foods to serve on Halloween, spookily decorated cakes, cookies and sweets are often enjoyed at parties. A growing tradition is to use the carved out pumpkin to make soup or pie.
- Bonfire night or Guy Fawkes Night marks the attempt to blow up the Houses of Parliament in 1605 and is celebrated on November 5th with fireworks and bonfires. Hot soups and stews along with sausages, Parkin, Toffee Apples and Bonfire Toffee are served to keep everyone warm whilst watching the festivities.

• Christmas is the biggest British celebration of the year. A religious festival that marks the birth of Jesus Christ, for many around the world it's also a time when families get together to enjoy festive meals and giving gifts.

Traditional yuletide foods are plentiful, from sweet dishes such as Mince Pies and Christmas Pudding and Brandy to the classic Christmas Roast Turkey or Roast Pheasant with all the trimmings, such as Yorkshire Puddings, Roast Potatoes and Brussels Sprouts. Christmas drinks include port, sherry and spicy Mulled Wine or Mulled Cider.

• Picnics are a great way to spend a lazy summer afternoon. Although the British weather is notoriously unpredictable, we still love eating outdoors! Home-made Scotch Eggs, Pork Pies and Potted Crab are perfect for simple al fresco meals along with delicious baked cakes, biscuits and fresh fruit salads. Ploughman's Lunch is also very popular for picnics or lazy lunches in pub gardens.

• Street parties are a very British innovation, held to commemorate momentous events in the past, such as VE day, or current events such as Royal weddings and jubilees. Trestle tables are set up along the street and everyone brings something to eat and share with their neighbours. Sandwiches, cold pies, quiches, salads, biscuits and cakes are just some of the favourites served.

• Barbecues have become increasingly popular in Britain over recent years. They are a great way to make the most of the long summer evenings and ideal for easy and informal entertaining with friends and family.

Sausages and burgers, along with marinated meat and fish, are perfect barbecue fare, served with fresh seasonal salads, such as Coleslaw or Coronation Chicken. A perfect accompaniment to a summer evening barbecue is a glass of English cider or scrumpy or some traditional British stout or ale.

Breakfast & Brunch

Full English Breakfast

SERVES 1

PREP TIME: 10 minutes

COOKING TIME: 15–20 minutes

nutritional information per serving	654 kcals, 46g fat, 13g sat fat, 8g total sugars, 4.2g salt

Famous around the world, this classic fry-up with egg, bacon, sausage, tomatoes, mushrooms and fried bread is the perfect start to the day. All you need for the perfect, complete meal is a steaming hot mug of tea!

INGREDIENTS

- 2 good quality pork sausages
- 2–3 rashers smoked back bacon
- 1 slice 2-day-old wholemeal bread
- 2 large tomatoes, halved
- vegetable oil, plus extra for drizzling
- 2–3 mushrooms
- 1 egg
- salt and pepper

1. Preheat the grill to high. Place the sausages under the hot grill and grill for about 15–20 minutes, turning frequently, until well browned.

2. Meanwhile, place the bacon rashers in a dry frying pan and fry for 2–4 minutes on each side. Remove from the frying pan, leaving all the excess bacon fat in the pan, and keep the bacon warm.

3. Heat the frying pan over a medium heat and place the bread in the fat. Cook for 1–2 minutes on one side, then turn over and repeat.

4. Place the tomato halves under the hot grill with the sausages. Drizzle with a little oil, season with salt and pepper to taste and grill for 3–4 minutes.

5. Add a little oil to a clean frying pan and fry the mushrooms. Remove from the pan and keep warm. Add the egg to the pan and fry, basting occasionally, for 1 minute, or until cooked to your liking.

6. Transfer the sausages, bacon, fried bread, tomatoes, mushrooms and egg to a plate and serve immediately.

4
5
5

Breakfast Omelette

SERVES 1

PREP TIME:
10 minutes

COOKING TIME:
20 minutes

nutritional information per serving	600 kcals, 49g fat, 17g sat fat, 5g total sugars, 3.6g salt

This is a delicious alternative way to serve a classic fried breakfast for one.

INGREDIENTS

- 2 tsp sunflower oil
- 1 Cumberland pork sausage
- 55 g/2 oz closed-cup mushrooms, wiped and sliced
- 2 rashers back bacon
- 2 large eggs
- 2 tbsp milk
- large knob of butter
- 1 tomato, thickly sliced
- pinch of dried thyme
- salt and pepper
- tomato ketchup and buttered toast, to serve

1. Heat the oil in a shallow frying pan or a medium-sized omelette pan and fry the sausage for 8–10 minutes until golden brown and cooked through, turning frequently. Remove and set aside on a plate lined with kitchen paper. Add the sliced mushrooms to the pan and fry over a high heat until golden brown. Set aside with the sausage.

2. Preheat the grill to medium and place the bacon rashers on the grill pan. Cook for 2–3 minutes on each side until crisp. Meanwhile, whisk the eggs and milk together in a jug and season with salt and pepper.

3. Wipe the pan clean and add the butter. Pour in the egg mixture and cook for 1–2 minutes until the egg is beginning to set. Using a fork, draw the cooked egg into the centre of the pan to allow the runny egg to run to the edges. Remove the pan from the heat when omelette is almost set. Thickly slice the sausage and place on the side of omelette with the bacon rashers, mushrooms and sliced tomato. Sprinkle with the thyme and pop under a hot grill for 1–2 minutes until sizzling. Slide the omelette onto a warmed plate, folding half of the omelette over the filling. Serve immediately with tomato ketchup and buttered toast.

1

2

3

SOMETHING DIFFERENT

For a vegetarian version, replace the sausage and bacon rashers with a few cooked new potatoes, sliced and fried until golden.

Potato Pancakes

SERVES 6

PREP TIME:
15 minutes

COOKING TIME:
10–15 minutes

nutritional information per serving	206 kcals, 6.5g fat, 1g sat fat, 2.5g total sugars, 0.9g salt

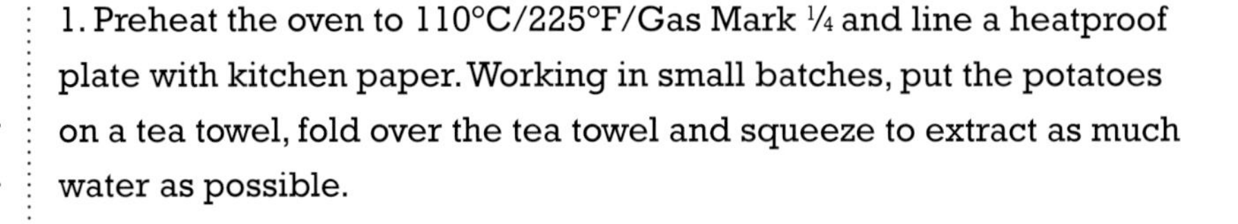
Serve these deliciously crisp potato cakes with a glass of sparkling Bucks Fizz for a special brunch.

INGREDIENTS

4 large potatoes, coarsely grated
1 large onion, grated
2 eggs, lightly beaten
55 g/2 oz fine matzo meal
1 tsp salt
pepper
sunflower oil, for frying

to serve
soured cream
thinly sliced smoked salmon
snipped chives

1. Preheat the oven to 110°C/225°F/Gas Mark ¼ and line a heatproof plate with kitchen paper. Working in small batches, put the potatoes on a tea towel, fold over the tea towel and squeeze to extract as much water as possible.

2. Put the potatoes in a large bowl, add the onion, eggs, matzo meal and the salt. Add the pepper to taste and mix together.

3. Heat a large, heavy-based frying pan over a medium-high heat. Add a thin layer of oil and heat until hot. Drop 2 tablespoons of the mixture into the pan and flatten slightly. Add as many more pancakes as will fit without overcrowding the pan. Fry for 2 minutes, or until crisp and golden underneath. Flip or turn with a palette knife and continue frying for a further 1–2 minutes, until crisp and golden.

4. Repeat using the remaining batter. Meanwhile, transfer the cooked pancakes to the prepared plate and keep warm in the oven. Add extra oil to the pan between batches, if necessary. Serve the pancakes hot, topped with soured cream and salmon and sprinkled with chives.

SOMETHING DIFFERENT

Instead of the smoked salmon, top the potato cakes with smoked mackerel or crab meat.

Devilled Kidneys

SERVES 2

PREP TIME:
15 minutes

COOKING TIME:
25–30 minutes

nutritional information per serving	258 kcals, 13.5g fat, 7.4g sat fat, 5g total sugars, 1.3g salt

This traditional breakfast dish dates back to Victorian times. Although it's rarely featured on breakfast menus nowadays, its strong, spicy flavours make this a really delicious weekend treat.

INGREDIENTS

6 lambs' kidneys
3 tbsp flour
1 tsp cayenne pepper
1 tsp English mustard powder
25 g/1 oz butter
1 onion, finely sliced
1 tbsp tomato purée
1 tbsp Worcestershire sauce
350 ml/12 fl oz chicken stock
salt and pepper
toasted wholemeal bread to serve

1. First prepare the kidneys by removing and discarding any membrane on the outside. Then run them under cold water and pat dry with kitchen paper. Cut each one in half and snip out the white cores with kitchen scissors. Cut the kidneys into chunky pieces.

2. Mix the flour, cayenne and mustard powder together in a shallow bowl and season with salt and pepper. Toss the kidney pieces lightly in the mixture to coat.

3. Melt the butter in a frying pan and cook the onion for 6–8 minutes until softened and starting to brown. Add the kidneys and cook for 2–3 minutes, turning regularly.

4. Stir in the tomato purée, the Worcestershire sauce, the stock, season with salt and pepper and simmer over gentle heat for 15 minutes.

5. Serve immediately on chunky toasted wholemeal bread.

1
2
3

Bacon Butties with Home-made Tomato Sauce

PREP TIME:
15 minutes

COOKING TIME:
25–30 minutes

nutritional information per serving	467 kcals, 25g fat, 11.5g sat fat, 10g total sugars, 2.9g salt

Nothing can beat a really good bacon sandwich and this is one of the best with a tangy home-made tomato sauce. Choose good quality smoked bacon and the freshest crusty white or brown bread.

INGREDIENTS

tomato sauce
(makes about 250 ml/9 fl oz)

2 tbsp olive oil
1 red onion, chopped
2 garlic cloves, chopped
250 g/9 oz plum tomatoes, chopped
250 g/9 oz canned chopped tomatoes
½ tsp ground ginger
½ tsp chilli powder
40 g/1½ oz dark brown sugar
100 ml/3½ fl oz red wine vinegar
salt and pepper

4 rashers smoked bacon
30 g/1 oz butter, softened
4 slices thick white or brown bread
pepper

1. To make the tomato sauce, heat the olive oil in a large saucepan and add the onion, garlic and tomatoes. Add the ginger and chilli and season with salt and pepper to taste. Cook for 15 minutes, or until soft.

2. Pour the mixture into a food processor and blend well. Sieve thoroughly to remove all the seeds. Return the mixture to the pan and add the sugar and vinegar. Return to the boil and cook until it is the consistency of ketchup.

3. Bottle quickly in sterilized bottles or jars and store in a cool place or refrigerator until ready to serve.

4. Place the rashers of bacon under a hot grill and grill, turning frequently until the bacon is crisp and golden brown. Spread the butter over the slices of bread.

5. Place two rashers on the base pieces of bread, season with pepper to taste and spoon or pour the sauce over the bacon. Top with the other slice of bread and serve immediately.

1
2
4

Scrambled Eggs on Waffles

SERVES 4

PREP TIME:
15 minutes

COOKING TIME:
15–20 minutes

nutritional information per serving	513 kcals, 33g fat, 15g sat fat, 4g total sugars, 1.5g salt

Home-made waffles are easy to make and taste great topped with creamy scrambled eggs.

INGREDIENTS

waffles

150 g/5½ oz plain white flour
1½ tsp baking powder
250 ml/9 fl oz milk
1 large egg
2 tbsp melted butter
4 tbsp finely chopped chives
sunflower oil, for greasing

scrambled eggs

8 eggs
4 tbsp single cream or milk
25 g/1 oz butter
salt and pepper
chives, to garnish

1. Sift the flour, baking powder and a pinch of salt into a bowl. Add the milk, egg, butter and chives and whisk to a smooth batter. Leave to stand for 5 minutes.

2. Lightly grease a waffle maker and heat until hot. Pour the batter into the waffle maker and cook until golden brown. Repeat, using the remaining batter, while keeping the cooked waffles warm.

3. For the scrambled eggs, beat the eggs with the cream and season to taste with salt and pepper. Melt the butter in a saucepan over a medium heat and add the egg mixture. Stir over a low heat until the eggs are lightly set but still creamy.

4. Serve the waffles immediately, topped with scrambled eggs, garnished with chives and seasoned with extra pepper.

1

3

3

COOK'S NOTE

Take care not to overcook the eggs or they will be dry and rubbery.

Courgette Fritters

MAKES 25

PREP TIME:
20 minutes

COOKING TIME:
30–40 minutes

nutritional information per fritter	28 kcals, 1g fat, 0.3g sat fat, 0.3g total sugars, 0.5g salt

Quick to make, fritters are ideal for a filling start to the day. To save time, you could prepare the batter the night before. Beat well before adding the courgettes, adding a little more milk if needed.

INGREDIENTS

100 g/3½ oz self-raising flour
2 eggs, beaten
50 ml/2 fl oz milk
300 g/10½ oz courgettes
2 tbsp fresh thyme
1 tbsp oil
salt and pepper

1. Sift the flour into a large bowl and make a well in the centre. Add the eggs to the well and, using a wooden spoon, gradually draw in the flour.

2. Slowly add the milk to the mixture, stirring constantly to form a thick batter.

3. Meanwhile, grate the courgettes over a sheet of kitchen paper placed in a bowl to absorb some of the juices.

4. Add the courgettes, thyme and salt and pepper to taste to the batter and mix thoroughly, for about a minute.

5. Heat the oil in a large, heavy-based frying pan. Taking a tablespoon of the batter for a medium-sized fritter or half a tablespoon of batter for a smaller-sized fritter, spoon the mixture into the hot oil and cook, in batches, for 3–4 minutes on each side.

6. Remove the fritters with a slotted spoon and drain thoroughly on absorbent kitchen paper. Keep each batch warm in the oven while making the rest. Transfer to serving plates and serve immediately.

1
3
5

Kippers with Poached Egg

SERVES 2 | PREP TIME: 5 minutes | COOKING TIME: 10 minutes

nutritional information per serving	426 kcals, 37g fat, 14g sat fat, 0.1g total sugars, 2.2g salt

Kippers take minutes to cook and taste great served with a poached egg and smothered in herb butter.

INGREDIENTS

- 2 large eggs
- 2 whole smoked kippers
- 40 g/1½ oz butter
- 1 tbsp fresh chopped parsley
- 1 tsp lemon juice
- salt and pepper
- lemon wedges, to garnish
- buttered wholemeal bread, to serve

1. Half fill a deep frying pan with boiling water and bring back to the boil. Reduce the heat to a gentle simmer. Break the eggs into the simmering water and poach for 2–3 minutes until the whites are set. Remove with a slotted spoon and drain on kitchen paper.

2. Add the kippers to the pan and simmer gently for 2–3 minutes until the flesh flakes easily. Meanwhile, place the butter in a small saucepan and heat until melted. Stir in the parsley and lemon juice and season with salt and pepper.

3. Remove the kippers from the pan and drain on kitchen paper. Place on two serving plates and top each with a poached egg. Spoon over the hot parsley butter and garnish with lemon wedges. Season with pepper and serve with buttered wholemeal bread.

COOK'S NOTE
Swirl the simmering water with a spoon before adding the eggs - this will help wrap the white around the yolk and give a good shape.

Eggy Bread

SERVES 2

PREP TIME:
10 minutes

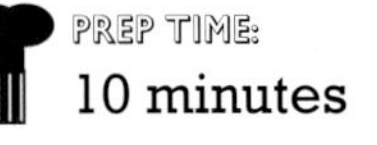
COOKING TIME:
5 minutes

nutritional information per serving	270 kcals, 18g fat, 10g sat fat, 3g total sugars, 0.9g salt

This family favourite is pure comfort food and children will love the messy business of dipping the slices of bread in the egg mixture! Serve sprinkled with brown sugar if you have a sweet tooth.

INGREDIENTS

1 large egg
4 tbsp milk or single cream
2 slices day-old thick white bread
30 g/1 oz butter

1. Break the egg into a shallow bowl and whisk well. Stir in the milk.

2. Dip the bread into the egg mixture and coat both sides well.

3. Heat half of the butter in a frying pan over a medium heat and gently fry one piece of eggy bread for about 1 minute on each side, or until golden brown and crispy. Take care not to let it burn. Remove from the pan and keep warm. Melt the remaining butter and repeat with the other piece of bread. Serve immediately.

GOES WELL WITH
Top with fresh fruit compote and Greek-style yogurt, drizzled with some honey.

Cheese & Parsley Muffins

MAKES 12

PREP TIME:
15 minutes

COOKING TIME:
20 minutes

nutritional information per muffin	154 kcals, 6.5g fat, 4g sat fat, 2g total sugars, 0.5g salt

For a breakfast on the go, these tasty savoury cheese and parsley muffins will fit the bill perfectly.

INGREDIENTS

- oil or melted butter, for greasing (if using)
- 280 g/10 oz plain flour
- 2 tsp baking powder
- ½ tsp bicarbonate of soda
- 25 g/1 oz smoked hard cheese, such as Applewood, grated
- 50 g/1¾ oz fresh parsley, finely chopped
- 1 egg
- 300 ml/10 fl oz thick natural yogurt
- 55 g/2 oz butter, melted and cooled

1. Preheat the oven to 200°C/400°F/Gas Mark 6. Grease a 12-cup muffin tin or line with 12 paper cases.

2. Sift together the flour, baking powder and bicarbonate of soda into a large bowl. Stir in the cheese and parsley.

3. Lightly beat the egg in a large jug, then beat in the yogurt and melted butter. Make a well in the centre of the dry ingredients and pour in the beaten liquid ingredients. Stir gently until just combined; do not over-mix.

4. Spoon the mixture into the prepared muffin tin. Bake in the preheated oven for 20 minutes, until well risen, golden brown and firm to the touch.

5. Leave the muffins in the tin for 5 minutes, then serve warm or transfer to a wire rack and leave to cool.

2

3

4

SOMETHING DIFFERENT Add a little finely chopped chilli for extra bite.

Smoked Salmon & Egg on Toasted Muffin

SERVES 2

PREP TIME:
20 minutes

COOKING TIME:
7–8 minutes

nutritional information per serving	918 kcals, 72g fat, 36g sat fat, 3g total sugars, 3.1g salt

Topped with an easy no-fail hollandaise sauce, this is the ultimate brunch dish.

INGREDIENTS

4 eggs
2 English muffins
butter, for spreading
15 g/½ oz rocket leaves
115 g/4 oz smoked salmon slices

hollandaise sauce
2 large egg yolks
2 tsp lemon juice
1 tbsp white wine vinegar
100 g/3½ oz unsalted butter
salt and pepper

1. To make the hollandaise sauce, place the egg yolks in a blender. Season with salt and pepper then process for a few seconds until thoroughly blended.

2. Place the lemon juice and white wine vinegar in a small saucepan and heat until simmering. With the blender running, slowly add the hot liquid in a steady stream. Turn the blender off.

3. Place the butter in the same saucepan and heat until melted and foaming. With the blender running, add the butter very slowly – a few drops at a time – until you have a smooth, thick sauce. Use a spatula to scrape down any of the sauce from the sides of the blender then whizz the sauce for a further few seconds.

4. Fill a deep frying pan with boiling water and bring back to the boil. Reduce the heat to a gentle simmer. Break the eggs into the water and poach for 2–3 minutes until the whites are set. Split and lightly toast the muffins under a hot grill.

5. Spread the toasted muffins with butter and place on two serving plates. Top with nearly all the rocket leaves and the slices of smoked salmon. Remove the eggs from the water with a slotted spoon, drain on kitchen paper then place on top of the salmon. Spoon the warm hollandaise sauce over the poached eggs. Garnish with black pepper and any remaining rocket leaves. Serve immediately.

1
2
5

Sardines on Toast

SERVES 4

PREP TIME:
20 minutes

COOKING TIME:
6–8 minutes

nutritional information per serving	319 kcals, 18g fat, 3.5g sat fat, 3.5g total sugars, 0.8g salt

Grilled fresh sardines and a peppery salad give this old-fashioned favourite a modern twist.

INGREDIENTS

4 fresh sardines (about 85 g/ 3 oz each), gutted, cleaned and heads removed

4 tbsp olive oil

4 slices sourdough or crusty bread

1 garlic clove, halved

200 g/7 oz cherry on-the-vine tomatoes, cut into bunches

40 g/1½ oz watercress

25 g/1 oz fresh flat-leaf parsley

1 tbsp balsamic vinegar

salt and pepper

1. To butterfly the sardines, lay them cut-side down on a board and press down along the backbone of each fish with your thumbs to loosen the bone. Turn each fish over and gently pull away the backbone. Cut the bone off at the tail end.

2. Season the sardines with salt and pepper and drizzle with a little of the olive oil. Preheat a grill to medium and grill the sardines for 3–4 minutes on each side until cooked through.

3. Meanwhile, heat a cast-iron frying or griddle pan until very hot. Rub the slices of bread with the cut garlic clove and brush with some of the remaining olive oil. Place on the hot pan with the tomato bunches. Cook the bread for 2–3 minutes on each side until lightly charred and the tomatoes for 4–5 minutes until just softened, turning frequently.

4. Place a cooked sardine on each chargrilled slice of bread. Mix the watercress and parsley together and pile on top of the sardines, then top with tomatoes. Whisk the rest of the olive oil with the balsamic vinegar and season. Drizzle over the dressing and serve immediately.

1

2

3

COOK'S NOTE

If there are any fine bones remaining in the flesh of the sardines after removing the main backbone, use tweezers to pull them out.

Eggs & Mustard Sauce with Pancakes

SERVES 4

PREP TIME: 15 minutes

COOKING TIME: 25–30 minutes

nutritional information per serving	778 kcals, 64g fat, 35g sat fat, 4g total sugars, 2g salt

This favourite breakfast dish is given an exciting new twist by serving the lightly poached eggs and buttery mustard sauce, with griddled pancakes instead of toasted muffins.

INGREDIENTS

pancakes

150 g/5½ oz plain white flour
1½ tsp baking powder
pinch of salt
250 ml/9 fl oz milk
1 large egg
2 tbsp melted butter
sunflower oil, for greasing

topping

4 large eggs
3 egg yolks
½ tsp English mustard
1 tbsp lemon juice
200 g/7 oz butter
salt and pepper

1. Sift the flour, baking powder and salt into a bowl. Add the milk, egg and butter and whisk to a smooth batter. Leave to stand for 5 minutes.

2. Lightly grease a griddle pan or frying pan and heat over a medium heat. Spoon tablespoons of batter onto the pan and cook until bubbles appear on the surface.

3. Turn over with a palette knife and cook the other side until golden brown. Repeat this process using the remaining batter, while keeping the cooked pancakes warm.

4. For the topping, bring a wide saucepan of water to the boil, then reduce the heat to a low simmer. Carefully break the eggs into the water and poach for about 2–3 minutes, until the whites are set but the yolks are still runny.

5. Meanwhile, place the egg yolks, mustard and lemon juice in a small bowl and stir to combine. Place the mixture in a blender and blend for a few seconds until smooth. Place the butter in a saucepan and heat until bubbling. With the motor running, gradually pour the butter into the egg yolks until the sauce is thickened and creamy. Season to taste with salt and pepper.

6. Serve immediately, in groups of three overlapping pancakes, with the eggs on top and the sauce spooned over and season with extra pepper.

4
5
5

Boiled Eggs with Soldiers

SERVES 2

PREP TIME:
5 minutes

COOKING TIME:
3–5 minutes

nutritional information per serving	444 kcals, 23g fat, 8g sat fat, 2g total sugars, 1.6g salt

A perfectly boiled egg with a runny yolk that spills out when dipped with a finger of toast is a truly classic British breakfast. For the best flavour, choose free-range organic eggs.

INGREDIENTS

4 large eggs
salt and pepper

soldiers
crusty white loaf, sliced and cut into thick fingers, buttered

1. Bring a small pan of water to the boil – it is useful to use a small pan to prevent the eggs rolling around too freely and cracking. The water should be deep enough to cover the eggs.

2. Gently lower the eggs into the water using a long-handled spoon. Keep the water at a gentle simmer and cook for 3–4 minutes for a runny yolk and set white, or 4–5 minutes for a firmer egg.

3. Remove the eggs from the pan using a slotted spoon, drain quickly on kitchen paper and place in egg cups.

4. Season with salt and pepper to taste and serve immediately with the soldiers.

1

2

3

COOK'S NOTE
Make sure the eggs are at room temperature - too cold and the shells may crack.

Breakfast Bloomer Loaf

MAKES
1 loaf

PREP TIME:
20 minutes plus proving

COOKING TIME:
40–45 minutes

nutritional information per loaf	2479 kcals, 33g fat, 16g sat fat, 14g total sugars, 11.7g salt

This traditional crusty loaf is ideal for breakfast - serve it thickly sliced, toasted if liked, with butter and marmalade.

INGREDIENTS

650 g/1 lb 7 oz strong plain flour, plus extra for dusting
2 tsp salt
2 tsp fast action dried yeast
25 g/1 oz butter, chilled and diced, plus extra for greasing
1 tsp caster sugar
400 ml/14 fl oz warm water
oil, for greasing

glaze

1 tbsp beaten egg
2 tsp milk

1. Lightly grease a large baking sheet. Mix the flour, salt and yeast in a large bowl. Add the butter and rub in to make fine breadcrumbs. Stir in the sugar. Make a well in the centre and pour in the warm water. Mix with a knife to make a soft, sticky dough.

2. Turn the dough onto a floured surface and knead for 10 minutes until smooth and elastic. Shape into a long oval loaf and place on the prepared baking sheet. Slash the top of the loaf six to seven times with a sharp knife. Cover loosely with lightly oiled clingfilm and leave in a warm place for 45–55 minutes until doubled in size. Preheat the oven to 230°C/450°F/Gas Mark 8.

3. To make the glaze, beat together the egg and milk with a fork. Lightly brush the glaze all over the loaf. Bake the loaf in the preheated oven for 10 minutes. Reduce the oven temperature to 200°C/400°F/ Gas Mark 6 and bake for a further 30–35 minutes, or until the loaf is golden brown and the base sounds hollow when tapped with your knuckles. Transfer to a wire rack to cool.

2

2

3

FREEZING TIP
Wrap in foil and freeze for up to 1 month. Thaw for 4-5 hours and refresh in a hot oven.

Sourdough Bread

MAKES
2 loaves

PREP TIME:
30 minutes plus starter and proving

COOKING TIME:
30 minutes

nutritional information per loaf	1271 kcals, 19g fat, 5g sat fat, 49g total sugars, 10.3g salt

This bread is made with a fermented batter-like 'starter' that gives it a unique flavour and wonderful texture.

INGREDIENTS

450 g/1 lb wholemeal flour
4 tsp salt
350 ml/12 fl oz warm water
2 tbsp black treacle
1 tbsp vegetable oil, plus extra for brushing
plain flour, for dusting

starter

85 g/3 oz wholemeal flour
85 g/3 oz strong white flour
55 g/2 oz caster sugar
250 ml/8 fl oz milk

1. For the starter, put the wholemeal flour, strong white flour, sugar and milk into a non-metallic bowl and beat well with a fork. Cover with a damp tea towel and leave to stand at room temperature for 4–5 days, until the mixture is frothy and smells sour.

2. Sift the flour and half the salt together into a bowl and add the water, treacle, oil and starter. Mix well with a wooden spoon until a dough begins to form, then knead with your hands until it leaves the side of the bowl. Turn out onto a lightly floured surface and knead for 10 minutes, until smooth and elastic.

3. Brush a bowl with oil. Form the dough into a ball, put it into the bowl and put the bowl into a polythene bag or cover with a damp tea towel. Leave to rise in a warm place for 2 hours, until the dough has doubled in volume.

4. Dust two baking sheets with flour. Mix the remaining salt with 4 tablespoons of water in a bowl. Turn out the dough on to a lightly floured work surface and knock back with your fist, then knead for a further 10 minutes. Halve the dough, shape each piece into an oval and place the loaves on the prepared baking sheets. Brush with some of the saltwater glaze and leave to stand in a warm place, brushing frequently with the glaze, for 30 minutes.

5. Preheat the oven to 220°C/425°F/Gas Mark 7. Brush the loaves with the remaining glaze and bake for 30 minutes, until the crust is golden brown and the loaves sound hollow when tapped on their bases with your knuckles. If it is necessary to cook them for longer, reduce the oven temperature to 190°C/375°F/Gas Mark 5. Transfer to wire racks to cool.

1
3
4

Granary Loaf

MAKES
1 loaf

PREP TIME:
20 minutes
plus proving

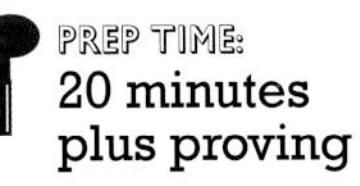

COOKING TIME:
30–35 minutes

nutritional information per loaf	1766 kcals, 31g fat, 4g sat fat, 16g total sugars, 7g salt

This wholesome granary loaf has a lovely nutty texture and flavour.

INGREDIENTS

500 g/1 lb 2 oz granary flour, plus extra for dusting
1½ tsp salt
2 tsp fast action dried yeast
2 tsp sunflower seeds
1 tbsp sunflower oil, plus extra for greasing
1 tsp runny honey
300 ml/10 fl oz warm water

1. Mix the granary flour, salt, yeast and the sunflower seeds in a large bowl and make a well in the centre. Mix together the oil, honey and warm water and pour into the bowl. Mix with a knife to make a soft, sticky dough.

2. Turn the dough onto a floured surface and knead for 10 minutes until smooth and elastic, adding a little more flour if the dough becomes too sticky. Place in a bowl, cover with lightly oiled clingfilm and leave in a warm place for 1–1½ hours until doubled in size. Preheat the oven to 220°C/425°F/Gas Mark 7. Lightly grease a 900 g/2 lb loaf tin.

3. Turn the dough onto a floured surface and knead again lightly for 1 minute. Shape into an oblong and place in the loaf tin. Cover with a clean damp tea towel and leave in a warm place for about 30 minutes until the dough has risen above the top of the edges of the tin. Dust the top of the loaf lightly with flour. Bake in the preheated oven for 30–35 minutes until golden brown and the loaf sounds hollow when tapped on the base with your knuckles. Transfer to a wire rack to cool.

2

2

3

GOES WELL WITH

Spread slices of toasted granary bread with soft cheese. Top with fresh peach slices, flaked almonds and a drizzle of maple syrup.

Cinnamon Swirls

MAKES 12

PREP TIME:
1 hour plus proving

COOKING TIME:
20–30 minutes

nutritional information per swirl	170 kcals, 8g fat, 4.5g sat fat, 9g total sugars, 0.3g salt

These swirls of buttery sweet bread with a cinnamon-spiced currant filling and a sticky maple syrup glaze taste delicious warm from the oven.

INGREDIENTS

225 g/8 oz strong white flour
½ tsp salt
2 tsp fast action dried yeast
2 tbsp butter, cut into small pieces, plus extra for greasing
1 egg, lightly beaten
125 ml/4 fl oz warm milk
2 tbsp maple syrup, for glazing

filling
4 tbsp butter, softened
2 tsp ground cinnamon
50 g/1¾ oz soft light brown sugar
50 g/1¾ oz currants

1. Grease a baking sheet with a little butter.

2. Sift the flour and salt into a mixing bowl. Stir in the yeast. Rub in the butter with your fingertips until the mixture resembles breadcrumbs. Add the egg and milk and mix to form a dough.

3. Form the dough into a ball, place in a greased bowl, cover and leave to stand in a warm place for about 40 minutes, or until doubled in size.

4. Lightly knock back the dough for 1 minute, then roll out to a rectangle measuring 30 x 23 cm/12 x 9 inches.

5. To make the filling, cream together the butter, cinnamon and sugar until light and fluffy. Spread the filling evenly over the dough rectangle, leaving a 2.5-cm/1-inch border all around. Sprinkle the currants evenly over the top.

6. Roll up the dough from one of the long edges, and press down to seal. Cut the roll into 12 slices. Place them, cut-side down, on the baking sheet, cover and leave to stand for 30 minutes.

7. Meanwhile, preheat the oven to 190°C/375°F/Gas Mark 5. Bake the buns in the preheated oven for 20–30 minutes, or until well risen. Brush with the maple syrup and leave to cool slightly before serving.

2
3
5

Apple & Cinnamon Pancakes

SERVES 4

PREP TIME:
20 minutes

COOKING TIME:
25–30 minutes

nutritional information per serving	360 kcals, 15g fat, 9g sat fat, 21g total sugars, 0.6g salt

These are great for feeding a crowd at breakfast time and everyone can join in making them!

INGREDIENTS

pancakes

150 g/5½ oz plain white flour
1 tsp ground cinnamon, plus extra for dusting
pinch of salt
250 ml/9 fl oz milk
100 ml/3½ fl oz apple juice
1 large egg
2 tbsp melted butter
butter, for frying

filling

3 apples, peeled and sliced
juice of ½ lemon
2 tbsp golden caster sugar

1. Sift the flour, cinnamon and salt into a bowl. Add the milk, apple juice, egg and butter and whisk to a smooth, bubbly batter. Leave to stand for 15 minutes.

2. For the filling, place the apples, lemon juice and sugar in a saucepan over a medium heat, cover and heat, stirring occasionally, until tender. Keep warm.

3. Put a small amount of the butter in a 20-cm/8-inch frying pan over a medium heat. Pour in enough batter to just cover the pan, swirling to cover in a thin, even layer. Cook until the underside is golden, then flip or turn with a palette knife and cook the other side until golden brown.

4. Repeat this process using the remaining batter. Interleave the cooked pancakes with kitchen paper and keep warm.

5. Spoon the apples onto the pancakes and fold over into fan shapes. Dust with cinnamon and serve immediately.

2

2

5

FREEZING TIP

Interleave the cooked pancakes with greaseproof paper, wrap and freeze for up to 1 month.

Muesli Pancakes with Honey

 SERVES 4

 PREP TIME: 15 minutes

COOKING TIME: 25–30 minutes

nutritional information per serving	385 kcals, 14g fat, 3.5g sat fat, 9g total sugars, 0.9g salt

Made with handy storecupboard ingredients, these lovely thick pancakes are full of muesli and flavoured with natural yogurt. Cooked with only a little fat and drizzled with honey, they make a nutritious start to the day.

INGREDIENTS

- 150 g/5½ oz plain white flour
- 1½ tsp baking powder
- pinch of salt
- 250 ml/9 fl oz milk
- 1 large egg
- 2 tbsp sunflower oil, plus extra for greasing
- 2 tbsp natural low-fat yogurt
- 140 g/5 oz muesli
- clear honey, to serve

1. Sift the flour, baking powder and salt into a bowl. Add the milk, egg, oil and yogurt and whisk to a smooth batter.

2. Stir in the muesli and leave to stand for 5 minutes. Lightly grease a griddle pan or frying pan and heat over a medium heat. Spoon tablespoons of batter onto the pan and cook until bubbles appear on the surface.

3. Turn over with a palette knife and cook the other side until golden brown. Repeat this process using the remaining batter, while keeping the cooked pancakes warm.

4. Spoon honey over the pancakes and serve immediately.

1

1

2

COOK'S NOTE

Choose a well-flavoured honey, such as heather, clover or acacia, to drizzle over the pancakes.

Porridge with Scotch

SERVES 4

PREP TIME:
25 minutes

COOKING TIME:
10 minutes

nutritional information per serving	337 kcals, 9.5g fat, 4g sat fat, 26g total sugars, 0.6g salt

This deluxe porridge is sweetened with honey and Scotch whisky syrup and topped with fresh raspberries.

INGREDIENTS

140 g/5 oz fresh raspberries
1½ tbsp icing sugar
1 tbsp orange juice
50 ml/2 fl oz Scotch whisky
3 tbsp heather honey
700 ml/1¼ pints milk
pinch of salt
115 g/4 oz rolled porridge oats

1. Place the raspberries in a bowl with the icing sugar and orange juice and stir well. Cover and leave for 15–20 minutes until the icing sugar has dissolved.

2. Place the Scotch and honey in a small saucepan and heat gently until the honey has dissolved. Bring to the boil and boil for 2–3 minutes until reduced and syrupy. Set aside.

3. To make the porridge, put the milk in a saucepan and bring to the boil. Stir in the salt and oats. Reduce the heat to low and simmer for 5–6 minutes, stirring frequently, until the porridge is thick and creamy. Stir in half the Scotch and honey syrup.

4. Spoon the porridge into bowls. Top with the raspberries and drizzle over the remaining Scotch and honey syrup.

HEALTHY HINT

For fewer calories, make porridge the traditional Scottish way with water instead of milk or use a mixture of the two.

Mixed Berry Muesli with Yogurt

PREP TIME:
15 minutes

COOKING TIME:
30–35 minutes

nutritional information per serving	334 kcals, 14g fat, 3g sat fat, 18.5g total sugars, 0.3g salt

Try this crunchy baked mix of oats, seeds, nuts and dried berries instead of your usual cereal.

INGREDIENTS

175 g/6 oz rolled porridge oats
25 g/1 oz pumpkin seeds
25 g/1 oz sunflower seeds
25 g/1 oz flaked almonds
1 tbsp sunflower oil
50 ml/2 fl oz maple syrup
50 ml/2 fl oz runny honey
25 g/1 oz dried sweetened cranberries
25 g/1 oz dried sweetened blueberries
300 g/10½ oz Greek-style yogurt
¼ tsp ground cinnamon
225 g/8 oz mixed berries (strawberries, raspberries and blueberries), to serve

1. Preheat the oven to 150°C/300°F/Gas Mark 2 and line a baking sheet with baking paper. Place the oats, seeds and flaked almonds in a large bowl. Mix together the oil, maple syrup and honey and pour over the oat mixture. Stir thoroughly.

2. Turn the mixture out onto a large baking sheet and spread it out evenly to a depth of approximately 1 cm/½ inch. Bake in the preheated oven for 30–35 minutes, until the mixture is golden brown.

3. Stir the mixture two to three times during baking either using a flat wooden spatula or metal fish slice. Remove from the oven and stir in the dried cranberries and blueberries. Leave the muesli to cool on the baking sheet.

4. To serve, divide the muesli between six serving bowls. Mix together the yogurt and cinnamon and spoon over the muesli. Serve topped with the fresh berries.

1

2

4

BE PREPARED

The muesli will keep stored in an airtight container for up to two weeks, so it's well worth making a double batch.

Sweet Waffles

SERVES 4

PREP TIME:
15 minutes

COOKING TIME:
25–30 minutes

nutritional information per serving	590 kcals, 24g fat, 14g sat fat, 21g total sugars, 1.6g salt

A variation on a classic but just as delicious, these buttery crisp waffles are ideal for an indulgent Sunday brunch.

INGREDIENTS

150 g/5½ oz plain white flour
1½ tsp baking powder
pinch of salt
1 tsp ground cinnamon
2 tbsp caster sugar
250 ml/9 fl oz milk
1 large egg
2 tbsp melted butter, plus extra to serve
sunflower oil, for greasing
8–10 slices brioche-type bread
demerara sugar, to serve

1. Sift the flour, baking powder, salt, cinnamon and sugar into a bowl. Add the milk, egg and butter and whisk to a smooth batter. Leave to stand for 5 minutes.

2. Lightly grease a waffle maker and heat until hot. Dip the slices of bread quickly into the batter, then place in the waffle maker and cook until golden brown. Repeat, using the remaining batter, while keeping the cooked waffles warm.

3. Serve immediately, with melted butter and sugar.

1

1

2

HEALTHY HINT

Instead of the butter and sugar, top with a large spoonful of fruit-flavoured yogurt.

Wholemeal Muffins

MAKES 10

PREP TIME: 20 minutes

COOKING TIME: 25–30 minutes

nutritional information per muffin	170 kcals, 5g fat, 0.7g sat fat, 10g total sugars, 0.4g salt

Muffins make the perfect breakfast or mid-morning treat. They're so quick to make you can have a batch on the table in under an hour!

INGREDIENTS

- 225 g/8 oz self-raising wholemeal flour
- 2 tsp baking powder
- 25 g/1 oz light muscovado sugar
- 100 g/3½ oz ready-to-eat dried apricots, finely chopped
- 1 banana, mashed with 1 tbsp orange juice
- 1 tsp orange rind, finely grated
- 300 ml/10 fl oz skimmed milk
- 1 egg, beaten
- 3 tbsp corn oil
- 2 tbsp porridge oats
- fruit spread, honey or maple syrup, to serve

1. Preheat the oven to 200°C/400°F/Gas Mark 6. Place 10 paper muffin cases in a muffin tin. Sift the flour and baking powder into a mixing bowl, adding any husks that remain in the sieve. Stir in the sugar and chopped apricots.

2. Make a well in the centre of the dry ingredients and add the banana, orange rind, milk, beaten egg and oil. Mix together well to form a thick batter. Divide the batter evenly among the 10 paper cases.

3. Sprinkle each muffin with a few porridge oats and bake in the preheated oven for 25–30 minutes, or until well risen and firm to the touch. Transfer the muffins to a wire rack to cool slightly. Serve the muffins warm with a little fruit spread, honey or maple syrup.

1

2

3

SOMETHING DIFFERENT

Add dried and sweetened cranberries or fresh blueberries or raspberries, if liked.

Lunch

Cream of Tomato Soup

COOKING TIME:
30–40 minutes

nutritional information per serving	224 kcals, 19g fat, 11g sat fat, 7g total sugars, 0.3g salt

This rich and creamy home-made soup made with ripe plum tomatoes and fragrant basil has all the flavour of summer. It's delicious served with warm crusty bread.

INGREDIENTS

25 g/1 oz butter
1 tbsp olive oil
1 onion, finely chopped
1 garlic clove, chopped
900 g/2 lb plum tomatoes, chopped
700 ml/1¼ pints vegetable stock
125 ml/4 fl oz dry white wine
2 tbsp sun-dried tomato purée
2 tbsp torn fresh basil leaves, plus extra leaves to garnish
150 ml/5 fl oz double cream
salt and pepper

1. Melt the butter with the oil in a large, heavy-based saucepan. Add the onion and cook, stirring occasionally, for 5 minutes, or until softened. Add the garlic, tomatoes, stock, wine and tomato purée, stir well and season to taste. Partially cover the saucepan and simmer, stirring occasionally, for 20–25 minutes, or until the mixture is soft and pulpy.

2. Remove the saucepan from the heat, leave to cool slightly, then pour into a blender or food processor. Add the torn basil and process. Push the mixture through a sieve into a clean saucepan with a wooden spoon.

3. Stir in the cream and reheat the soup, but do not let it boil. Ladle the soup into warmed bowls, garnish with the basil leaves and serve immediately.

1

2

2

FREEZING TIP

Freeze for up to 2 months in plastic containers. Thaw for 3-4 hours then reheat gently.

Winter Vegetable Soup

PREP TIME:
15 minutes

nutritional information per serving	163 kcals, 4g fat, 0.5g sat fat, 9g total sugars, 0.8g salt

A hearty, chunky vegetable soup makes a wonderful warming lunch for the winter months. This simple recipe is packed with root vegetables, flavoured with garlic and topped with grated cheese – it'll soon become a family favourite.

INGREDIENTS

- 2 tbsp vegetable oil
- 1 large onion, thickly sliced
- 1 large potato, cut into chunks
- 3 celery sticks, thickly sliced
- 4 carrots, sliced
- 175 g/6 oz swede, cut into chunks
- 4 large garlic cloves, peeled and left whole
- 1.5 litres/2¾ pints chicken or vegetable stock
- 225 g/8 oz canned chopped tomatoes
- 1 leek, halved lengthways and thickly sliced
- salt and pepper
- 2 tbsp chopped fresh flat-leaf parsley, to garnish
- grated Cheddar cheese, to serve

1. Heat the oil in a large, heavy-based saucepan over a medium heat. Add the onion, potato, celery, carrots, swede and garlic cloves. Season to taste with salt and pepper, then cover and cook over a medium heat, stirring occasionally, for 10 minutes.

2. Pour in the stock and tomatoes and bring to the boil. Reduce the heat and simmer, partially covered, for 30 minutes. Add the leek and cook for a further 5 minutes, until just tender.

3. Taste and adjust the seasoning, adding salt and pepper if needed. Ladle into warmed bowls, garnish with the parsley and serve immediately with grated Cheddar cheese.

1
2
3

Scotch Broth

SERVES 8

PREP TIME:
15 minutes
plus chilling

COOKING TIME:
2 hours

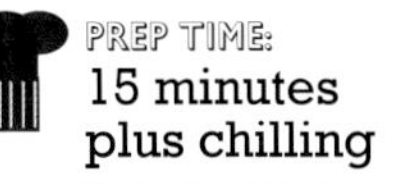

nutritional information per serving	191 kcals, 7.5g fat, 3g sat fat, 5.5g total sugars, 0.2g salt

This classic soup is simmered gently to allow the lamb, vegetables and pearl barley to become meltingly tender.

INGREDIENTS

700 g/1 lb 9 oz neck of lamb
1.7 litres/3 pints water
55 g/2 oz pearl barley
2 onions, chopped
1 garlic clove, finely chopped
3 small turnips, diced
3 carrots, finely sliced
2 celery sticks, sliced
2 leeks, sliced
salt and pepper
2 tbsp chopped fresh parsley, to garnish

1. Cut the meat into small pieces, removing as much fat as possible. Put into a large saucepan and cover with the water. Bring to the boil over a medium heat and skim off any foam that appears.

2. Add the pearl barley, reduce the heat and cook gently, covered, for 1 hour.

3. Add the onion, garlic and vegetables and season with salt and pepper to taste. Continue to cook for a further hour. Remove from the heat and allow to cool slightly.

4. Remove the meat from the saucepan using a slotted spoon and strip the meat from the bones. Discard the bones and any fat or gristle. Place the meat back in the saucepan and leave to cool thoroughly, then refrigerate overnight.

5. Scrape the solidified fat off the surface of the soup. Reheat, season with salt and pepper to taste and ladle into bowls. Serve immediately, garnished with the parsley.

1

2

3

GOES WELL WITH

Wedges of warm buttered soda bread are the perfect accompaniment for this hearty soup.

Ham & Cheese Toastie

MAKES 1

PREP TIME:
5 minutes

COOKING TIME:
4–6 minutes

nutritional information per sandwich	592 kcals, 38g fat, 23g sat fat, 2.5g total sugars, 3.1g salt

Strong flavoured cheese and a slice of ham combine to give a wonderful melting middle to this hot sandwich. Serve with a lightly dressed crisp green salad for a more substantial lunch.

INGREDIENTS

- 2 slices country-style bread, such as white crusty bread, thinly sliced
- 20 g/¾ oz butter, at room temperature
- 55 g/2 oz Cheddar cheese, grated
- 1 slice cooked ham, trimmed to fit the bread, if necessary

1. Thinly spread each slice of bread on one side with butter, then put one slice on the work surface, buttered side down. Sprinkle half the cheese over, taking it to the edge of the bread, then add the ham and top with the remaining cheese.

2. Add the other slice of bread, buttered side up, and press down. Heat a heavy-based frying pan, ideally non-stick, over a medium-high heat until hot. Reduce the heat to medium, add the sandwich and fry on one side for 2–3 minutes, until golden brown.

3. Flip the sandwich over and fry on the other side for 2–3 minutes, until all the cheese is melted and the bread is golden brown. Cut the sandwich in half diagonally and serve immediately.

COOK'S NOTE
For extra flavour, spread the bread with a little English or wholegrain mustard.

Steak & English Mustard Sandwich

 SERVES 2

 PREP TIME: 15 minutes

COOKING TIME: 25 minutes

nutritional information per serving	799 kcals, 49g fat, 12g sat fat, 6.5g total sugars, 2.1g salt

Crusty bread, chargrilled peppered steak, sweet caramelized onions and mustard mayo combine to make this the ultimate sandwich!

INGREDIENTS

- 15 g/½ oz butter
- 3 tbsp olive oil
- 1 onion, halved and thinly sliced
- ½ tsp brown sugar
- 2 rump steaks, each about 175 g/6 oz weight and 2 cm/¾ inch thick
- 1 tsp coarsely ground black pepper
- 4 tbsp mayonnaise
- 2 tsp ready-made English mustard
- 4 thick slices crusty white bread
- 25 g/1 oz rocket leaves
- salt and pepper

1. Heat the butter and half the oil in a frying pan and fry the sliced onion gently for 10 minutes until softened. Season with salt and pepper and sprinkle over the sugar. Increase the heat a little and continue cooking for a further 5 minutes until golden and caramelized.

2. Heat a cast-iron griddle pan until very hot. Drizzle the remaining oil over the steaks, coat with the black pepper and season lightly with salt. Add the steaks to the pan and cook over a high heat for 3–5 minutes on each side, until cooked to your liking. Remove the steaks from the pan, cover and leave to rest in a warm place for 10 minutes.

3. Mix together the mayonnaise and mustard and spread thickly over two slices of the bread. Top with the rocket leaves. Using a sharp knife, thinly slice the steaks on an angle. Pile the steak on top of the rocket leaves and top with the caramelized onions. Sandwich with the remaining slices of bread, halve and serve immediately.

1

2

3

COOK'S NOTE

Remove the steaks from the fridge and leave at room temperature for at least 20 minutes before cooking.

Mushroom & Onion Quiche

SERVES 4

PREP TIME:
50 minutes
plus chilling

COOKING TIME:
45 minutes

nutritional information per serving	552 kcals, 45g fat, 22g sat fat, 5g total sugars, 0.6g salt

This deluxe quiche has a delicious filling of red onions, earthy wild mushrooms and fresh thyme.

INGREDIENTS

butter, for greasing
200 g/7 oz shortcrust pastry
flour, for dusting

filling

55 g/2 oz unsalted butter
3 red onions, halved and sliced
350 g/12 oz mixed wild mushrooms, such as ceps, chanterelles and morels
2 tsp chopped fresh thyme
1 egg
2 egg yolks
100 ml/3½ fl oz double cream
salt and pepper

1. Preheat the oven to 190°C/375°F/Gas Mark 5. Lightly grease a 23-cm/9-inch loose-based quiche tin. Roll out the dough on a lightly floured work surface and use to line the tin. Line the pastry case with baking paper and fill with baking beans. Chill in the refrigerator for 30 minutes. Bake in the preheated oven for 25 minutes. Remove the paper and beans and cool on a wire rack. Reduce the oven temperature to 180°C/350°F/Gas Mark 4.

2. To make the filling, melt the butter in a large, heavy-based frying pan over a very low heat. Add the onions, cover and cook, stirring occasionally, for 20 minutes. Add the mushrooms and thyme and cook, stirring occasionally, for a further 10 minutes. Spoon into the pastry case and put the tin on a baking sheet.

3. Lightly beat the egg, egg yolks, cream and salt and pepper to taste in a bowl. Pour over the mushroom mixture. Bake in the oven for 20 minutes, or until the filling is set and golden. Serve hot or at room temperature.

1

2

3

SOMETHING DIFFERENT

Add a splash of dry sherry or red wine to the pan when frying the onions.

Pork & Pickle Pie

SERVES 10

PREP TIME:
20 minutes
plus chilling

COOKING TIME:
1 hour 15 minutes

nutritional information per serving	647 kcals, 41g fat, 18g sat fat, 4g total sugars, 2.1g salt

A simpler version of a classic pork pie, this tasty pie is ideal for a summer picnic.

INGREDIENTS

pastry

450 g/1 lb plain flour, plus extra for dusting

115 g/4 oz butter, chilled and diced, plus extra for greasing

115 g/4 oz white vegetable fat, chilled and diced

7–8 tbsp cold water

salt

milk, to glaze

filling

800 g/1 lb 12 oz good quality pork sausages, skins removed and roughly chopped

400 g/14 oz pork shoulder, coarsely minced

85 g/3 oz fresh white breadcrumbs

2 tbsp chopped fresh parsley

4 spring onions, trimmed and finely chopped

4 tbsp pickle

salt and pepper

1. To make the pastry, sift the flour and a pinch of salt into a bowl. Add the butter and white vegetable fat and rub in with fingertips until the mixture resembles fine breadcrumbs. Sprinkle over the cold water and mix to a firm dough. Wrap in clingfilm and chill in the refrigerator for 30 minutes.

2. To make the filling, place the sausages, pork shoulder, breadcrumbs, parsley and spring onions in a bowl and mix thoroughly. Season with salt and pepper. Preheat the oven to 200°C/400°F/Gas Mark 6. Grease a 23-cm/9-inch round springform tin.

3. Roll two thirds of the pastry out on a floured surface to a 33-cm/13-inch circle and use to line the prepared tin. Trim the edges. Press half the pork mixture into the pastry case. Spread over the pickle then top with the rest of the pork mixture.

4. Roll out the remaining pastry to a 23-cm/9-inch circle. Brush the rim of the pastry in the tin with water then top with the pastry circle, crimping the edges together firmly to seal. Cut leaves from the pastry trimmings and attach them to the pie with water.

5. Glaze the pie with the milk and pierce two holes in the pastry to allow the steam to escape. Place the tin on a lipped baking sheet. Bake in the preheated oven for 30 minutes then reduce the oven temperature to 180°C/350°F/Gas Mark 4 and bake for a further 45 minutes. Cool in the tin for 30 minutes then unclip the tin and leave the pie to cool on the base. Serve warm or cold.

1
2
3

Cornish Pasties

PREP TIME:
20 minutes
plus chilling

COOKING TIME:
50 minutes

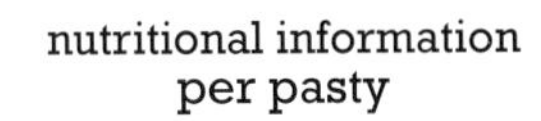

nutritional information per pasty	968 kcals, 57g fat, 29g sat fat, 4g total sugars, 0.7g salt

These world-famous pasties were originally made for Cornish tin miners to take to work for a filling lunch.

INGREDIENTS

pastry

- 400 g/14 oz plain flour, plus extra for dusting
- 100 g/3½ oz butter, chilled and diced, plus extra for greasing
- 100 g/3½ oz white vegetable fat, chilled and diced
- 4–5 tbsp cold water
- 1 egg beaten with 1 tbsp water
- salt

filling

- 115 g/4 oz swede, thinly sliced and chopped
- 175 g/6 oz potatoes, thinly sliced and chopped
- 1 small onion, finely chopped
- 280 g/10 oz beef skirt or rump steak, finely chopped
- 25 g/1 oz butter, melted
- 2 tsp plain flour
- salt and pepper

1. To make the pastry, sift the flour and a large pinch of salt into a large bowl. Add the butter and white vegetable fat and rub in with your fingertips until the mixture resembles fine breadcrumbs. Add enough of the cold water to mix to a firm dough. Cut into four even-sized pieces and wrap in clingfilm and chill in the refrigerator for 15 minutes. Preheat the oven to 220°C/425°F/Gas Mark 7. Lightly grease a large baking sheet or line with baking paper.

2. Roll each piece of pastry out on a lightly floured surface to a 20-cm/8-inch circle. For the filling, layer the swede, potatoes and onion on one half of each of the pastry circles. Season with salt and pepper then top with the chopped beef and season again. Dot the butter over the beef and sprinkle with the flour.

3. Brush the rim of each pastry circle with water then fold the pastry over to enclose the filling. Seal and crimp the edges tightly. Place the pasties on the prepared baking sheet and glaze with the egg mixture.

4. Bake in the preheated oven for 20 minutes. Remove the baking sheet from the oven and glaze the pasties with the egg mixture again. Reduce the oven temperature to 190°C/375°F/Gas Mark 5 and bake the pasties for a further 30 minutes until golden brown. Transfer to a wire rack to cool before serving.

1
2
3

Game Pie

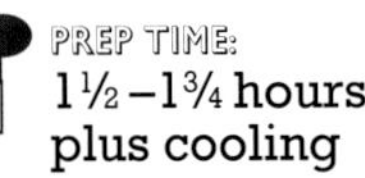

1½–1¾ hours plus cooling

COOKING TIME:
30–35 minutes

nutritional information per serving	654 kcals, 33g fat, 13g sat fat, 8g total sugars, 1.6g salt

This rich pie is perfect for an autumn supper or festive meal. Choose whatever mix of game is available at the time.

INGREDIENTS

- 2 tbsp sunflower oil
- 800 g/1 lb 12 oz boneless mixed game (such as venison, rabbit and pheasant), cut into 2.5-cm/1-inch cubes
- 225 g/8 oz shallots, halved
- 1 garlic clove, chopped
- 100 g/3½ oz smoked bacon lardons
- 175 g/6 oz carrots, chopped
- 2 tbsp flour, plus extra for dusting
- 300 ml/10 fl oz chicken stock
- 200 ml/7 fl oz red wine
- 2 tbsp redcurrant jelly
- few sprigs of fresh thyme
- 500 g/1 lb 2 oz puff pastry
- salt and pepper
- beaten egg, to glaze

1. Heat half of the oil in a large flameproof casserole dish. Fry the game meat in batches until brown, then remove with a slotted spoon and set aside. Add the rest of the oil to the dish and fry the shallots, garlic, bacon and carrots for 10 minutes, stirring, until browned.

2. Add the flour to the dish and cook for one minute then stir in the stock, red wine and redcurrant jelly and bring to the boil. Return the game meat to the dish with the thyme sprigs. Season with salt and pepper then cover and simmer very gently for 1–1¼ hours, or until the meat is tender. Leave to cool for 1 hour.

3. Preheat the oven to 220°C/425°F/Gas Mark 7. Transfer the game casserole to a large oval pie dish and place a pie funnel in the centre of the dish. Dampen the rim of the dish with cold water.

4. Roll out the pastry on a lightly floured surface to an oval at least 5 cm/2 inches wider all round than the dish. Cut a 2.5-cm/1-inch strip of pastry from the outer edge, brush with water and use to line the rim of the dish. Brush the pastry rim with water and top with the oval pastry lid. Seal, trim and crimp the pastry edges and decorate the top of the pie with pastry trimmings, if liked.

5. Glaze the pie with the beaten egg. Bake in the preheated oven for 30–35 minutes until the pastry is risen and golden. Serve immediately.

1
1
2

Steak, Ale & Kidney Pudding

SERVES 4

PREP TIME:
35 minutes
plus cooling

COOKING TIME:
4½ hours

nutritional information per serving	864 kcals, 47g fat, 22g sat fat, 4.5g total sugars, 1.8g salt

Great for a warming winter supper, this traditional favourite is comfort food at its best.

INGREDIENTS

filling

600 g/1 lb 5 oz chuck or braising steak, cut into 2.5-cm/1-inch cubes

225 g/8 oz beef or lambs' kidney, trimmed and cut into 1-cm/½-inch cubes

2 tbsp seasoned flour

25 g/1 oz butter, plus extra for greasing

2–3 tbsp sunflower oil

1 large onion, chopped

225 ml/8 fl oz brown ale

350 ml/12 fl oz beef stock

1 bouquet garni

115 g/4 oz brown cap mushrooms, quartered

suet pastry

225 g/8 oz self-raising flour, plus extra for dusting

100 g/3½ oz suet

½ tsp salt

1 tsp dried mixed herbs

approx 150 ml/5 fl oz cold water

1. Preheat the oven to 150°C/300°F/Gas Mark 2. Toss the meat in the seasoned flour. Heat the butter and half the oil in a flameproof casserole dish and fry the meat in batches, until browned. Set aside.

2. Add the remaining oil to the casserole dish and fry the onion for 5 minutes. Stir in the ale and stock and bring to the boil. Return the meat to the pan with the bouquet garni. Cover and cook in the preheated oven for 2 hours. Stir in the mushrooms and leave to cool. Remove the bouquet garni.

3. To make the suet pastry, sift the flour into a large bowl and stir in the suet, salt and dried mixed herbs. Stir in enough of the cold water to make a soft dough. Grease a 1.4-litre/2½-pint pudding basin.

4. Roll out three quarters of the pastry on a floured surface to a thickness of 15 mm/⅝ inch and use to line the prepared pudding basin, allowing the excess pastry to hang slightly over the edges.

5. Using a slotted spoon, transfer the meat mixture into the basin. Pour in some of the gravy to almost cover the meat (reserve the rest). Roll out the remaining pastry to make a lid. Place the pastry lid over the filling, brush the pastry edges with water and fold over to seal. Cover with pleated, greased, greaseproof paper and foil and secure with string. Steam the pudding in a covered saucepan half-filled with water for 2½ hours, topping the pan up with boiling water if necessary.

6. Allow to cool slightly then uncover the pudding and turn out onto a plate. Heat through the reserved gravy to serve with the pudding.

1
4

Sausage Rolls

PREP TIME: 30 minutes

COOKING TIME: 20–25 minutes

nutritional information per roll	300 kcals, 18.6g fat, 7.6g sat fat, 1.1g total sugars, 1g salt

These crisp and golden sausage rolls are flavoured with fresh chopped sage, onion and wholegrain mustard.

INGREDIENTS

- 2 tsp sunflower oil
- 1 small onion, finely chopped
- 2 tsp chopped fresh sage
- 450 g/1 lb pork sausage meat
- 2 tsp wholegrain mustard
- 25 g/1 oz fresh white breadcrumbs
- 350 g/12 oz ready-rolled puff pastry
- salt and pepper
- 1 egg beaten with 1 tbsp water, to glaze

1. Heat the oil in a frying pan and gently fry the chopped onion for 8–10 minutes until soft and pale golden. Transfer to a large bowl, stir in the chopped sage and leave to cool. Preheat the oven to 200°C/400°F/Gas Mark 6.

2. Add the sausage meat to the bowl with the mustard and breadcrumbs. Season with salt and pepper and mix thoroughly with a fork.Unroll the pastry sheet and cut in half lengthways. Divide the sausage meat mixture into two equal portions and lay along the length of each strip of pastry in a cylinder shape.

3. Brush one long edge of each strip of pastry with some of the egg and water mixture and fold over the pastry to enclose the filling. Press the edges together well to seal and cut each roll into four shorter lengths. Lightly dampen a large baking sheet with cold water and place the sausage rolls on it, spaced well apart. Glaze the pastry with the egg and water mixture. Bake in the preheated oven for 20–25 minutes until crisp and golden. Transfer to a wire rack and serve warm or cold.

1

2

3

FREEZING TIP

Freeze the unbaked sausage rolls for up to one month. Thaw at room temperature for 4–5 hours then bake as per the recipe.

Ploughman's Lunch

SERVES 4

PREP TIME:
15 minutes
plus cooling

COOKING TIME:
10 minutes

nutritional information per serving	670 kcals, 48g fat, 23g sat fat, 8.5g total sugars, 2.7g salt

Perfect for al fresco entertaining, this classic pub platter is easy to assemble and serve. Look for good quality, local ingredients when you shop.

INGREDIENTS

4 large eggs

225 g/8 oz British cheese, such as farmhouse Cheddar cheese, Stilton and/or Somerset brie

300 g/10½ oz ready-made pork pie

1 carrot

8 spring onions

16 baby vine tomatoes

4 slices of cured, sliced ham

4 tbsp chutney of your choice

85 g/3 oz salad leaves

crusty bread, to serve

1. First, boil the eggs. Bring a small pan of water to the boil. Gently lower the eggs into the water using a long-handled spoon. Keep the water at a gentle simmer and cook for 6–8 minutes, or until cooked to your liking. Remove the eggs using a slotted spoon and drain quickly on kitchen paper. Leave to cool.

2. When the eggs are cool enough to handle, remove and discard the shells. Cut the eggs in half. Cut the cheese into wedges and the pork pie into quarters. Cut the carrot into batons and trim the spring onions.

3. Arrange all the ingredients on individual serving plates. Serve immediately, accompanied by crusty bread.

GOES WELL WITH

Serve with a jug of chilled home-made lemonade or iced beers for the grown ups!

Welsh Rarebit

SERVES 4

PREP TIME:
10 minutes

COOKING TIME:
10–15 minutes

nutritional information per serving	390 kcals, 27g fat, 16g sat fat, 1.5g total sugars, 1.6g salt

This traditional savoury dish dates back to the 18th century and was considered to be a luxurious supper in those days. It's still a delicious treat and makes a great light lunch or late night snack.

INGREDIENTS

- 4 thick slices brown bread
- 225 g/8 oz mature Cheddar cheese, grated
- 25 g/1 oz butter
- 3 tbsp beer
- ½ tsp mustard powder
- 1 egg, beaten
- salt and pepper

1. Toast the bread under a medium grill on one side only.

2. Put the cheese into a saucepan and add the butter and beer. Heat slowly over a low heat, stirring continuously. Add some salt and pepper and the mustard powder and stir well until the mixture is thick and creamy. Remove from the heat and leave to cool slightly before mixing in the egg. Preheat the grill to high.

3. Spread the rarebit generously over the untoasted side of the bread and place under a hot grill until golden and bubbling. Serve immediately.

SOMETHING DIFFERENT Replace the beer with cider and top with apple chutney.

Bubble & Squeak

SERVES 4

PREP TIME:
10 minutes

COOKING TIME:
35–40 minutes

nutritional information per serving	332 kcals, 23g fat, 9g sat fat, 8g total sugars, 0.3g salt

So named because of the noise made in the pan as the vegetables are fried, this tasty dish can be made with leftover cooked vegetables or cooked from scratch. Serve with grilled meat or a lightly poached egg.

INGREDIENTS

450 g/1 lb floury potatoes, such as King Edward, Maris Piper or Desirée, cut into chunks
55 g/2 oz butter
3 tbsp hot milk
450 g/1 lb green cabbage
4 tbsp olive oil
1 onion, thinly sliced
salt and pepper

1. Bring a large saucepan of lightly salted water to the boil, add the potatoes and cook for 15–20 minutes. Drain well and mash with a potato masher until smooth. Season with salt and pepper, add the butter and milk and stir well.

2. Cut the cabbage into quarters, remove the stalk and finely shred the leaves.

3. Heat half of the oil in a large frying pan, add the onion and fry until soft. Add the cabbage to the pan and stir-fry for 2–3 minutes until soft. Season with salt and pepper, add the potato and mix together well.

4. Press the mixture firmly into the frying pan and leave to cook over a high heat for 4–5 minutes until the base is crispy. Place a plate over the pan and invert the pan so that the potato cake falls onto the plate. Add the remaining oil to the pan, reheat and slip the cake back into the pan with the uncooked side down.

5. Continue to cook for a further 5 minutes until the base is crispy. Turn out onto a warmed plate and cut into wedges for serving. Serve immediately.

1
3
4

Chicken Liver Pâté

 SERVES 6

 PREP TIME: 20 minutes plus chilling

COOKING TIME: 10–15 minutes

nutritional information per serving	413 kcals, 42g fat, 26g sat fat, 0.9g total sugars, 0.6g salt

A quick and easy pâte with a lovely smooth texture and rich flavour.

INGREDIENTS

- 200 g/7 oz butter
- 225 g/8 oz trimmed chicken livers, thawed if frozen
- 2 tbsp Marsala wine or brandy
- 1½ tsp chopped fresh sage
- 1 garlic clove, roughly chopped
- 150 ml/5 fl oz double cream
- salt and pepper
- fresh bay leaves or sage leaves, to garnish
- Melba toast, to serve

1. Melt 40 g/1½ oz of the butter in a large, heavy-based frying pan. Add the chicken livers and cook over a medium heat for 4 minutes on each side. They should be brown on the outside but still pink in the centre. Transfer to a food processor and process until finely chopped.

2. Stir the Marsala into the frying pan, scraping up any sediment with a wooden spoon, then add to the food processor with the chopped sage, garlic and 100 g/3½ oz of the remaining butter. Process until smooth. Add the cream, season to taste and process until thoroughly combined and smooth. Spoon the pâté into a dish or individual ramekins, smooth the surface and leave to cool completely.

3. Melt the remaining butter in a small saucepan, allow to cool for 5 minutes, skim off any white froth then spoon over the surface of the pâté, leaving any sediment in the saucepan. Garnish with herb leaves, leave to cool, then cover and chill in the refrigerator. Serve with Melba toast.

2

2

3

Scotch Eggs

PREP TIME: 25 minutes

COOKING TIME: 10-15 minutes

nutritional information per serving	511 kcals, 35g fat, 8g sat fat, 0.7g total sugars, 1.5g salt

These picnic favourites are a world away from shop-bought ones and well worth the time and effort it takes to make them.

INGREDIENTS

- 4 large hard-boiled eggs
- 300 g/10½ oz good quality sausage meat
- 1 tbsp plain flour, plus a little more for shaping
- 1 egg, beaten
- 100 g/3½ oz fresh breadcrumbs
- vegetable oil, for deep-frying
- salt and pepper
- mixed green salad, to serve

1. Cool the eggs under cold running water. Peel carefully and wipe to make sure there are no pieces of shell attached to the eggs.

2. Divide the sausage meat into four equal portions and flatten out into rounds on a floured surface – they should be large enough to enclose the eggs.

3. Mix the flour with the salt and pepper to taste and put on a plate.

4. Put the beaten egg in a small bowl and the fresh breadcrumbs into a larger bowl.

5. Drop the eggs, one at a time, into the flour and then work the sausage meat around each egg until they are a good shape and have a smooth appearance. Brush with beaten egg and then toss in the breadcrumbs until evenly coated.

6. Heat the oil in a deep fat fryer to 150°C/300°F or in a heavy-based saucepan, checking the temperature with a thermometer. Fry the eggs for 6–8 minutes until they are golden brown. Remove them from the pan and drain well on kitchen paper. If using a saucepan, only cook two of the Scotch eggs at a time to be safe.

7. Cool completely, slice the Scotch eggs in half and serve immediately with a green salad.

2
4
5

Potted Crab

SERVES 4

PREP TIME:
20 minutes
plus chilling

COOKING TIME:
2 minutes

nutritional information per serving	351 kcals, 34g fat, 20g sat fat, 0.2g total sugars, 1.1g salt

Full of the flavour of the sea, this buttery crab pâte is ideal for a simple summer lunch or starter.

INGREDIENTS

- 140 g/5 oz cooked white crabmeat
- 85 g/3 oz cooked brown crabmeat
- ¼ tsp cayenne pepper
- 2 tbsp lemon juice
- 150 g/5½ oz butter, softened
- salt and pepper
- fresh parsley sprigs, to garnish
- lemon wedges and Melba toast or crusty bread, to serve

1. Place the white and brown crabmeat in a bowl and mix together with a fork. Stir in the cayenne pepper and lemon juice and season with salt and pepper.

2. Add 85 g/3 oz of the butter and beat until thoroughly combined. Divide the mixture between four 125-ml/4-fl oz ramekin dishes and level the surface.

3. Place the remaining butter in a small saucepan and heat gently until melted. Cool for 5 minutes then skim off any white froth with a spoon. Pour the melted butter in a thin stream over the top of each pot of crab mixture to cover evenly, leaving any sediment in the base of the pan. Leave until cold then place the ramekins in the refrigerator for about 2 hours until the butter is firm.

4. Remove the ramekins from the refrigerator about 30 minutes before serving. Garnish with parsley sprigs and serve with lemon wedges and Melba toast or crusty bread.

1

2

3

Filo-wrapped Asparagus

SERVES 6

PREP TIME:
15 minutes

COOKING TIME:
15 minutes

nutritional information per serving	455 kcals, 42g fat, 17g sat fat, 4g total sugars, 1g salt

Make the most of the short early summer English asparagus season with this simple and stylish recipe. Served with a creamy basil and garlic dip, it's perfect for a special light lunch or a dinner party starter.

INGREDIENTS

- 18 plump asparagus spears, tough ends snapped off
- 3 sheets filo pastry, each measuring about 45 x 24 cm/17¾ x 9½ inches
- 125 g/4½ oz butter, melted, plus extra for greasing
- 90 g/3¼ oz freshly grated Parmesan cheese
- salt

dip

- 150 ml/5 fl oz good quality mayonnaise
- 150 ml/5 fl oz natural yogurt
- 10–12 fresh basil leaves, torn into small pieces
- 1 garlic clove, crushed (optional)

1. Blanch the asparagus in a saucepan of lightly salted boiling water for 30–40 seconds, then transfer to a bowl of cold water using a slotted spoon. Drain and pat dry with kitchen paper.

2. Preheat the oven to 200°C/400°F/Gas Mark 6. Lay one sheet of the filo pastry on a work surface, covering the remaining sheets with a damp tea towel to prevent them from drying out. Brush the sheet of filo with a little of the melted butter and sprinkle with one third of the Parmesan, then cut into six rectangles, each measuring about 15 x 12 cm/6 x 4½ inches.

3. Place an asparagus spear at one end of each rectangle and roll up. Transfer to a lightly greased baking sheet. Repeat with the remaining pastry, Parmesan and asparagus. Brush with the remaining butter and bake in the preheated oven for 12–14 minutes, until crisp and golden brown.

4. To make the dip, mix together the mayonnaise, yogurt, basil and garlic, if using, in a small bowl. Serve the filo-wrapped asparagus warm or cold with the dip.

1
1
2

Corned Beef Hash

SERVES 2

PREP TIME: 10 minutes

COOKING TIME: 25–30 minutes

nutritional information per serving	473 kcals, 27g fat, 13g sat fat, 10g total sugars, 2.5g salt

Corn beef hash became more popular during World War Two, when fresh meat was heavily rationed.

INGREDIENTS

- 1 large potato, cubed
- 25 g/1 oz butter
- 1 tbsp extra virgin olive oil
- 1 small onion, chopped
- 140 g/5 oz cooked beetroot without vinegar, cubed
- 200 g/7 oz canned corned beef, cubed
- salt
- 1 tbsp chopped fresh parsley, to garnish
- horseradish sauce, to serve

1. Cook the potato in a saucepan of lightly salted boiling water for 10–15 minutes, or until just tender. Meanwhile, in a large, heavy-based frying pan, melt the butter with the oil and cook the onion for 5 minutes, or until soft.

2. Drain the potato and add to the frying pan. Add the beetroot and cook, stirring occasionally, for 5 minutes. Stir in the corned beef and flatten the mixture with a spatula. Increase the heat and cook the mixture, without stirring, for 3 minutes or until heated through.

3. Loosen the sides and base of the cake with the spatula, shaking the pan. Place a plate over the top of the cake and, while pressing the plate down onto the cake with one hand, flip the pan over in one action and let the cake drop onto the plate. Garnish with the parsley and serve, with horseradish sauce on the side.

SOMETHING DIFFERENT

Replace the corned beef with leftover roast beef from the Sunday lunch.

Prawn Cocktail with Quail Eggs

PREP TIME: 20 minutes

COOKING TIME: 5 minutes

nutritional information per serving	340 kcals, 28.5g fat, 6g sat fat, 3.5g total sugars, 1.6g salt

This deluxe version of a British favourite is made with large and juicy king prawns, avocado and quail eggs.

INGREDIENTS

- 8 quail eggs
- 6 tbsp mayonnaise
- 3 tbsp Greek-style yogurt
- 2 tbsp tomato ketchup
- dash of Tabasco sauce
- 2 tsp lime juice
- 40 g/1½ oz peppery salad leaves
- 5-cm/2-inch piece of cucumber, finely diced
- 1 small ripe avocado, peeled and thinly sliced
- 225 g/8 oz cooked king prawns, peeled and tails left intact
- salt and pepper
- lime wedges and fresh dill sprigs, to garnish

1. Bring a small saucepan of water to the boil then reduce to a simmer. Gently lower the quail eggs into the water and simmer for 5 minutes. Drain and cool under running cold water. Once cold, shell and set aside.

2. Place the mayonnaise, yogurt, ketchup, Tabasco sauce and lime juice in a bowl and mix together thoroughly. Season to taste with salt and pepper.

3. Divide the salad leaves between four large wine or cocktail glasses. Scatter over the diced cucumber. Halve the eggs and arrange on top of the salad with the avocado slices and prawns (reserving eight prawns to garnish).

4. Spoon over the mayonnaise dressing. Serve garnished with the reserved prawns, lime wedges and sprigs of dill.

1

2

3

COOK'S NOTE

Remove the quail eggs from the refrigerator at least 30 minutes before cooking to allow them to come to room temperature, otherwise they will take longer to cook.

Garden Salad

SERVES 4

PREP TIME:
10–15 minutes

COOKING TIME:
No cooking

nutritional information per serving	61 kcals, 1g fat, 0.4g sat fat, 7g total sugars, trace salt

A lovely salad with fresh vegetables and a creamy herb dressing – it's a real taste of summer!

INGREDIENTS

½ romaine or cos lettuce
½ cucumber, thinly sliced
6 spring onions, thinly sliced
100 g/3½ oz peas, thawed if frozen
1 courgette
croûtons, to serve

dressing
100 ml/3½ fl oz natural low-fat yogurt
juice of ½ lemon
2 tsp clear honey
2 tbsp snipped chives
salt and pepper

1. Roughly tear or shred the lettuce and place in a large salad bowl with the cucumber, onions and peas.

2. Use a vegetable peeler to slice the courgette into long thin ribbons and add to the bowl.

3. To make the dressing, use a fork to blend together the yogurt, lemon juice and honey in a small bowl. Stir in the chives and season to taste with salt and pepper.

4. Drizzle the dressing over the salad and toss well to mix evenly. Sprinkle croûtons over the top of the salad and serve immediately.

1

2

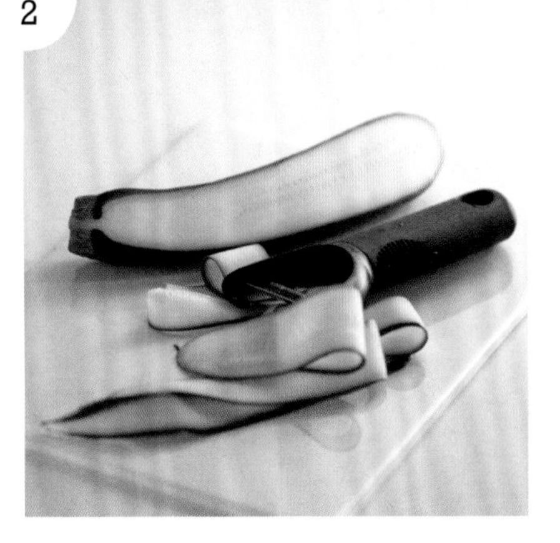

3

COOK'S NOTE
If fresh peas are available, use them instead of frozen – there's no need to cook them.

Coronation Chicken

SERVES 4

PREP TIME:
20 minutes

COOKING TIME:
20–25 minutes

nutritional information per serving	366 kcals, 21g fat, 12g sat fat, 11g total sugars, 0.6g salt

Created for the Queen's Coronation in 1953, this is a modern version of a true British classic.

INGREDIENTS

450 g/1 lb skinless chicken fillets
a few black peppercorns
1 bay leaf
150 g/5½ oz crème fraîche
6 tbsp Greek-style yogurt
2 tsp mild curry paste
1 tbsp smooth mango chutney
1 tbsp lemon juice
2 tbsp chopped fresh coriander
4 ready-to-eat dried apricots, chopped
1 small ripe mango, peeled, stone removed and thinly sliced
125 g/4½ oz baby salad leaves
25 g/1 oz cashew nuts, lightly toasted
salt and pepper
fresh coriander leaves, to garnish
mini poppadoms, to serve (optional)

1. Place the chicken fillets in a deep frying pan with the peppercorns and bay leaf. Cover with cold water and bring to the boil. Reduce the heat, cover and simmer for 15–20 minutes until the chicken is cooked through. Turn off the heat and leave the chicken to cool in the liquid.

2. Place the crème fraîche, yogurt and curry paste in a bowl and beat together until smooth. Stir in the mango chutney, lemon juice and coriander and season to taste with salt and pepper.

3. Drain the chicken from the cooking liquid and tear into short strips. Gently toss in the curried dressing with the apricots and nearly all the mango slices.

4. Arrange the salad leaves on a platter or four individual serving plates. Spoon the chicken mixture on top with the remaining mango slices. Scatter over the cashew nuts, garnish with fresh coriander leaves and serve with mini poppadoms, if liked.

1
2
3

Coleslaw

SERVES 12

PREP TIME:
15–20 minutes

COOKING TIME:
No cooking

nutritional information per serving	123 kcals, 10g fat, 2g sat fat, 6g total sugars, 0.2g salt

Home-made coleslaw made with crisp cabbage, carrots and peppers in a creamy, lightly spiced dressing is so much better than shop bought. Add a handful of raisins or some thinly sliced apple to give a sweeter flavour.

INGREDIENTS

150 ml/5 fl oz mayonnaise
150 ml/5 fl oz natural yogurt
dash of Tabasco sauce
1 head of white cabbage
4 carrots
1 green pepper
salt and pepper

1. Mix the mayonnaise, yogurt, Tabasco sauce, and salt and pepper to taste together in a small bowl. Chill in the refrigerator until required.

2. Cut the cabbage in half and then into quarters. Remove and discard the tough centre stalk. Finely shred the cabbage leaves. Wash the leaves under cold running water and dry thoroughly on kitchen paper. Roughly grate the carrots or shred in a food processor or on a mandoline. Quarter and deseed the green pepper and cut the flesh into thin strips.

3. Mix the vegetables together in a large serving bowl and toss to mix. Pour over the dressing and toss until the vegetables are well coated. Cover and chill in the refrigerator until required.

1

2

3

GOES WELL WITH

You can add in plenty of other ingredients, to add taste, colour and texture, such as capers, apples, sunflower and pumpkin seeds.

Devils & Angels on Horseback

MAKES 32

PREP TIME:
15 minutes

COOKING TIME:
10–15 minutes

nutritional information per piece	54 kcals, 3.5g fat, 1g sat fat, 2g total sugars, 0.7g salt

These popular canapés are great for lunchtime entertaining – easy to make and simple to serve.

INGREDIENTS

devils

8 rindless lean bacon rashers
8 canned anchovy fillets in oil, drained
16 whole blanched almonds
16 ready-to-eat prunes

angels

8 rindless lean bacon rashers
16 smoked oysters, drained if canned

sprigs of fresh thyme, to garnish

1. Preheat the oven to 200°C/400°F/Gas Mark 6.

2. For the devils, cut each bacon rasher lengthways in half and gently stretch with the back of a knife. Cut each anchovy fillet lengthways in half. Wrap half an anchovy around each almond and press them into the cavity where the stones have been removed from the prunes. Wrap a strip of bacon around each prune and secure with a cocktail stick.

3. For the angels, cut each bacon rasher lengthways in half and gently stretch with the back of a knife. Wrap a bacon strip around each oyster and secure with a cocktail stick.

4. Put the devils and angels onto a baking sheet and cook in the preheated oven for 10–15 minutes until sizzling hot and the bacon is cooked. Garnish with sprigs of fresh thyme and serve hot.

2

2

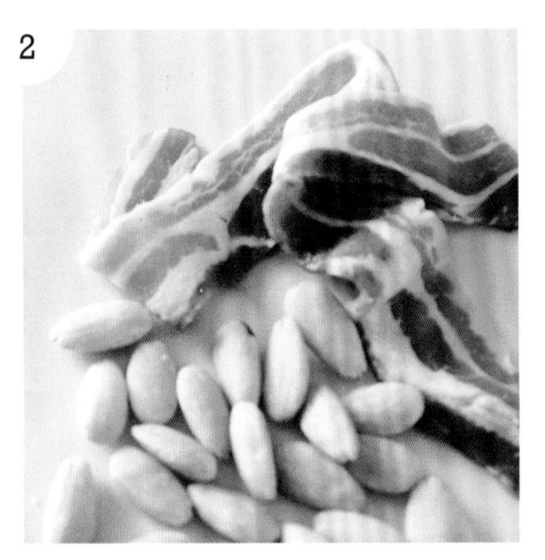

2

BE PREPARED

Make and chill in the refrigerator up to four hours in advance, then bake when required.

Afternoon Tea

Date & Walnut Loaf

SERVES 8

PREP TIME:
30 minutes

COOKING TIME:
35–40 minutes

nutritional information per serving	204 kcals, 9g fat, 4g sat fat, 17g total sugars, 0.3g salt

Soaking the fruit in hot tea gives this simple cake a lovely moist texture and fantastic flavour.

INGREDIENTS

- 100 g/3½ oz dates, stoned and chopped
- ½ tsp bicarbonate of soda
- finely grated rind of ½ lemon
- 100 ml/3½ fl oz hot tea
- 40 g/1½ oz unsalted butter, plus extra for greasing
- 70 g/2½ oz light muscovado sugar
- 1 small egg
- 125 g/4½ oz self-raising flour
- 25 g/1 oz walnuts, chopped
- walnut halves, to decorate

1. Preheat the oven to 180°C/350°F/Gas Mark 4. Grease a 450-g/1-lb loaf tin and line with baking paper.

2. Place the dates, bicarbonate of soda and lemon rind in a bowl and add the hot tea. Leave to soak for 10 minutes until softened.

3. Cream the butter and sugar together until light and fluffy, then beat in the egg. Stir in the date mixture.

4. Fold in the flour using a large metal spoon, then fold in the walnuts. Spoon the mixture into the prepared cake tin and smooth the surface. Top with the walnut halves.

5. Bake in the preheated oven for 35–40 minutes or until risen, firm and golden brown. Cool for 10 minutes in the tin, then turn out onto a wire rack to cool completely.

2

3

4

GOES WELL WITH

Beat a teaspoon of ground cinnamon into softened butter to spread on the slices.

Lemon Drizzle Cake

SERVES 8

PREP TIME:
20 minutes

COOKING TIME:
45–60 minutes

nutritional information per serving	426 kcals, 21g fat, 5g sat fat, 33g total sugars, 0.4g salt

This cake has a tangy lemon sugar syrup drizzled over it while still warm which permeates through the sponge to give it a wonderful moistness and extra lemony flavour.

INGREDIENTS

butter, for greasing
200 g/7 oz plain flour
2 tsp baking powder
200 g/7 oz caster sugar
4 eggs
150 ml/5 fl oz soured cream
grated rind of 1 large lemon
4 tbsp lemon juice
150 ml/5 fl oz sunflower oil

syrup
4 tbsp icing sugar
3 tbsp lemon juice

1. Preheat the oven to 180°C/350°F/Gas Mark 4. Grease a 20-cm/8-inch loose-bottomed round cake tin and line with baking paper.

2. Sift the flour and baking powder into a mixing bowl and stir in the caster sugar.

3. In a separate bowl, whisk the eggs, soured cream, lemon rind, lemon juice and oil together.

4. Pour the egg mixture into the dry ingredients and mix well until evenly combined.

5. Pour the mixture into the prepared tin and bake in the preheated oven for 45–60 minutes, or until risen and golden brown.

6. Meanwhile, to make the syrup, mix together the icing sugar and lemon juice in a small saucepan. Stir over a low heat until just beginning to bubble and turn syrupy.

7. As soon as the cake comes out of the oven, prick the surface with a fine skewer, then brush the syrup over the top. Leave the cake to cool completely in the tin before turning out and serving.

2
3
4

Gingerbread

SERVES 12

PREP TIME:
30 minutes
plus cooling

COOKING TIME:
1–1¼ hours

nutritional information per serving	298 kcals, 10g fat, 5.5g sat fat, 35g total sugars, 0.6g salt

The flavour of this cake will improve with time. If you have the patience, wrap the un-iced cake in greaseproof paper and store in a cool place for a few days before icing.

INGREDIENTS

250 g/9 oz plain flour
1 tsp bicarbonate of soda
1½ tsp ground ginger
1 tsp ground mixed spice
115 g/4 oz butter, plus extra for greasing
115 g/4 oz light muscovado sugar
150 g/5½ oz golden syrup
85 g/3 oz black treacle
2 large eggs, beaten
2 tbsp milk

icing

115 g/4 oz icing sugar
1 tbsp stem ginger syrup
1–2 tbsp water
1 piece stem ginger, finely chopped

1. Preheat the oven to 160°C/325°F/Gas Mark 3. Grease an 18-cm/7-inch square cake tin and line with baking paper.

2. Sift the flour, bicarbonate of soda, ground ginger and mixed spice into a large bowl. Place the butter, sugar, golden syrup and black treacle in a saucepan and heat gently, stirring all the time, until the butter has melted. Cool for 5 minutes.

3. Stir the melted mixture into the bowl and mix well. Add the eggs and milk and beat until thoroughly incorporated.

4. Spoon the mixture into the prepared tin and bake in the preheated oven for 1–1¼ hours, or until well risen and firm to the touch. Cool in the tin for 15 minutes then turn out onto a wire rack to cool completely.

5. For the icing, sift the icing sugar into a bowl. Stir in the stem ginger syrup and enough of the water to make a smooth icing that just coats the back of a wooden spoon.

6. Spoon the icing over the top of the cake, allowing it to run down the sides. Scatter over the stem ginger and leave to set.

2
4
6

Chocolate Chip Sponge Cake

COOKING TIME:
40–45 minutes

nutritional information per serving	592 kcals, 36g fat, 19g sat fat, 41g total sugars, 0.9g salt

This sponge cake is made by the quick all-in-one method. This is where all the ingredients are beaten together until smooth and creamy.

INGREDIENTS

- 225 g/8 oz self-raising flour
- ½ tsp baking powder
- 225 g/8 oz butter, softened, plus extra for greasing
- 225 g/8 oz caster sugar
- 55 g/2 oz ground almonds
- 4 eggs
- 1 tsp vanilla extract
- 140 g/5 oz milk chocolate chips
- 55 g/2 oz milk or plain chocolate, melted, to decorate
- 55 g/2 oz white chocolate, melted, to decorate

1. Preheat the oven to 180°C/350°F/Gas Mark 4. Grease a 23-cm/9-inch square shallow cake tin and line with baking paper.

2. Sift the flour and baking powder into a large bowl. Add the butter, sugar, ground almonds, eggs and vanilla extract. Using an electric handheld whisk, beat until the mixture is very smooth and creamy. Fold in half the chocolate chips.

3. Spoon the mixture into the prepared cake tin and gently smooth the surface. Scatter over the rest of the chocolate chips. Bake in the preheated oven for 40–45 minutes, or until well risen, golden and springy to the touch.

4. Leave the cake to cool in the tin for 5 minutes, then turn out onto a wire rack to cool completely.

5. To decorate, spoon the melted chocolates into two separate paper piping bags. Snip off the ends and drizzle the chocolates in squiggly lines over the cake. Leave to set. Cut into squares and serve.

2
3
5

Fruit Cake

SERVES 16

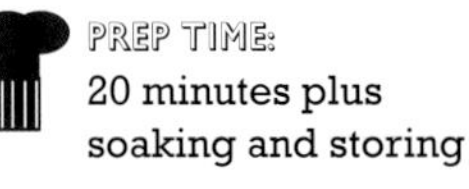
PREP TIME:
20 minutes plus soaking and storing

COOKING TIME:
2¼–2¾ hours

nutritional information per serving	400 kcals, 15.5g fat, 8g sat fat, 51g total sugars, 0.2g salt

The cake of choice for celebrations, such as weddings and Christmas, this classic favourite should be made well in advance to allow time for the rich flavours to mature.

INGREDIENTS

350 g/12 oz sultanas
225 g/8 oz raisins
115 g/4 oz ready-to-eat dried apricots, chopped
85 g/3 oz dates, stoned and chopped
4 tbsp dark rum or brandy, plus extra for flavouring (optional)
finely grated rind and juice of 1 orange
225 g/8 oz unsalted butter, plus extra for greasing
225 g/8 oz light muscovado sugar
4 eggs
70 g/2½ oz chopped mixed peel
85 g/3 oz glacé cherries, quartered
25 g/1 oz chopped glacé ginger or stem ginger
40 g/1½ oz blanched almonds, chopped
200 g/7 oz plain flour
1 tsp ground mixed spice

1. Place the sultanas, raisins, apricots and dates in a large bowl and stir in the rum, orange rind and orange juice. Cover and leave to soak for several hours or overnight.

2. Preheat the oven to 150°C/300°F/Gas Mark 2. Grease a 20-cm/8-inch round deep cake tin and line with baking paper.

3. Beat the butter and sugar together until light and fluffy. Gradually beat in the eggs, beating hard after each addition. Stir in the soaked fruits, mixed peel, glacé cherries, glacé ginger and blanched almonds.

4. Sift the flour and mixed spice, then fold lightly and evenly into the mixture. Spoon the mixture into the prepared cake tin and smooth the surface, making a slight depression in the centre with the back of the spoon.

5. Bake in the preheated oven for 2¼–2¾ hours, or until the cake is beginning to shrink away from the sides and a skewer inserted into the centre comes out clean. Cool completely in the tin.

6. Turn out the cake and remove the lining paper. Wrap in greaseproof paper and foil, and store for at least two months before use. To add a richer flavour, prick the cake with a skewer and spoon over a couple of extra tablespoons of rum or brandy, if using, before storing.

1
3
4

Cherry & Almond Loaves

MAKES 12

PREP TIME:
15 minutes
plus cooling

COOKING TIME:
20–25 minutes

nutritional information per loaf	183 kcals, 11g fat, 4.5g sat fat, 14g total sugars, 0.2g salt

So dainty, these small loaves are just right with tea when you don't want anything too rich or filling.

INGREDIENTS

- 85 g/3 oz salted butter, softened, plus extra for greasing
- 70 g/2½ oz caster sugar
- 1 egg
- 1 egg yolk
- 70 g/2½ oz self-raising flour
- ½ tsp almond extract
- 55 g/2 oz ground almonds
- 55 g/2 oz glacé cherries, roughly chopped
- 2 tbsp flaked almonds

icing

- 55 g/2 oz icing sugar
- 2 tsp lemon juice

1. Preheat the oven to 180°C/350°F/Gas Mark 4. Place a 12-section silicone mini loaf sheet on a baking sheet, or grease and line individual mini loaf tins with baking paper. Put the butter, caster sugar, egg, egg yolk, flour, almond extract and ground almonds in a mixing bowl and beat together with an electric handheld whisk until smooth and creamy. Stir in the cherries.

2. Using a teaspoon, spoon the mixture into the tray sections and level with the back of the spoon. Break up the flaked almonds slightly by squeezing them in your hands and scatter them over the cake mixture. Bake in the preheated oven for 20 minutes (25 minutes if using tins), or until risen and just firm to the touch. Leave in the tray for 5 minutes, then transfer to a wire rack to cool.

3. Beat the icing sugar and lemon juice together in a small bowl and drizzle over the cakes with a teaspoon. Leave to set.

1

2

3

SOMETHING DIFFERENT
Replace the cherries with dried cranberries or apricots.

Iced Madeira Cake

SERVES 10

PREP TIME:
30 minutes plus cooling

COOKING TIME:
1–1¼ hours

nutritional information per serving	388 kcals, 17g fat, 10g sat fat, 36g total sugars, 0.2g salt

Named after the wine it was traditionally served with, this classic sponge cake has a fairly firm texture with a buttery flavour. Topped with a tangy lemon icing, it makes the perfect teatime treat.

INGREDIENTS

175 g/6 oz unsalted butter, softened, plus extra for greasing
175 g/6 oz caster sugar
finely grated rind of 1 lemon
3 eggs, lightly beaten
140 g/5 oz self-raising flour
115 g/4 oz plain flour
2 tbsp milk
1 tbsp lemon juice

icing

175 g/6 oz icing sugar
2–3 tbsp lemon juice
2 tsp lemon curd, warmed

1. Preheat the oven to 160°C/325°F/Gas Mark 3. Grease a 900-g/2 lb loaf tin and line with baking paper.

2. Place the butter and caster sugar in a large bowl and beat together until very pale and fluffy. Beat in the lemon rind then gradually beat in the eggs.

3. Sift the self-raising and plain flour into the mixture and fold in gently until thoroughly incorporated. Fold in the milk and lemon juice.

4. Spoon the mixture into the prepared tin and bake in the preheated oven for 1–1¼ hours, or until well risen, golden brown and a skewer inserted into the centre comes out clean. Cool in the tin for 15 minutes, then turn out onto a wire rack to cool completely.

5. For the icing, sift the icing sugar into a bowl. Add the lemon juice and stir to make a smooth and thick icing. Gently spread the icing over the top of the cake. Drizzle the warmed lemon curd over the icing and drag a skewer through the icing to create a swirled effect. Leave to set.

2
4
5

Bakewell Tart

SERVES 6

PREP TIME:
30 minutes
plus chilling

COOKING TIME:
40 minutes

nutritional information per serving	607 kcals, 38g fat, 18g sat fat, 30g total sugars, 0.6g salt

This tart is a version of the traditional Bakewell pudding named after the Derbyshire town. It has a crisp pastry case filled with a layer of jam and is topped with almond frangipane and flaked almonds.

INGREDIENTS

pastry

150 g/5½ oz plain flour, plus extra for dusting

85 g/3 oz butter, cut into small pieces, plus extra for greasing

35 g/1¼ oz icing sugar, sifted

finely grated rind of ½ lemon

½ egg yolk, beaten

1½ tbsp milk

filling

4 tbsp strawberry jam

100 g/3½ oz butter

100 g/3½ oz soft light brown sugar

2 eggs, beaten

1 tsp almond extract

75 g/2¾ oz ground rice

3 tbsp ground almonds

3 tbsp flaked almonds, toasted

icing sugar, for dusting

1. To make the pastry, sift the flour into a bowl. Rub in the butter with your fingertips until the mixture resembles fine breadcrumbs. Mix in the icing sugar, lemon rind, egg yolk and milk.

2. Knead briefly on a lightly floured work surface. Wrap the dough in clingfilm and chill in the refrigerator for 30 minutes.

3. Preheat the oven to 190°C/375°F/Gas Mark 5. Grease a 20-cm/ 8-inch flan tin. Roll out the pastry to a thickness of 5 mm/¼ inch and use it to line the base and side of the tin. Prick all over the base with a fork, then spread with the jam.

4. To make the filling, cream the butter and sugar together until fluffy. Gradually beat in the eggs, followed by the almond extract, ground rice and almonds. Spread the mixture evenly over the jam-covered pastry, then sprinkle over the flaked almonds. Bake in the preheated oven for 40 minutes, until golden. Remove from the oven, dust with icing sugar and serve immediately.

Pear & Chocolate Squares

PREP TIME:
30 minutes

COOKING TIME:
1–1¼ hours

nutritional information per square	273 kcals, 15g fat, 7g sat fat, 20g total sugars, 0.4g salt

These rich almond and chocolate sponge squares have a delicious layer of fresh chopped pear through the middle.

INGREDIENTS

- 140 g/5 oz wholemeal plain flour
- 140 g/5 oz self-raising flour
- 175 g/6 oz butter, diced, plus extra for greasing
- 100 g/3½ oz ground almonds
- 85 g/3 oz caster sugar
- 450 g/1 lb firm ripe pears, peeled, cored and roughly chopped
- 2 large eggs, separated
- 25 g/1 oz cocoa powder
- 2 tsp baking powder
- 175 g/6 oz soft dark brown sugar
- 5 tbsp milk

1. Preheat the oven to 180°C/350°F/Gas Mark 4. Grease an 18-cm/7-inch square deep cake tin and line with baking paper. Sift the wholemeal and self-raising flours into a bowl. Add the butter and rub in with your fingertips until the mixture resembles fine breadcrumbs.

2. Transfer 25 g/1 oz of the mixture to a separate bowl. Add the ground almonds, caster sugar, pears and the white of one egg to the remaining mixture. Mix well.

3. Sift the cocoa powder and baking powder together. Stir into the remaining butter mixture with the brown sugar. Add the remaining egg white, egg yolks and milk. Mix well.

4. Spread half of the chocolate mixture over the base of the prepared cake tin. Spread the pear mixture over the top. Cover with the remaining chocolate mixture and smooth the surface. Bake in the preheated oven for 1–1¼ hours or until risen and the centre is firm to the touch. Leave to cool in the tin then turn out and cut into squares.

1

3

4

SOMETHING DIFFERENT
Replace the chopped pears with peeled and chopped apples or ripe peaches.

Rhubarb, Raisin & Ginger Muffins

MAKES 12

PREP TIME: 20 minutes

COOKING TIME: 15–20 minutes

nutritional information per muffin	214 kcals, 11g fat, 6g sat fat, 14g total sugars, 0.4g salt

Tart fresh rhubarb and spicy stem ginger are the perfect partners for these deliciously different muffins.

INGREDIENTS

- oil or melted butter, for greasing (if using)
- 250 g/9 oz rhubarb
- 200 g/7 oz plain flour
- 2 tsp baking powder
- 115 g/4 oz caster sugar
- 2 eggs
- 100 ml/3½ fl oz milk
- 125 g/4½ oz butter, melted and cooled
- 3 tbsp raisins
- 2 pieces of stem ginger in syrup, drained and chopped

1. Preheat the oven to 180°C/350°F/Gas Mark 4. Grease a 12-cup muffin tin or line with 12 paper cases. Chop the rhubarb into 1-cm/½-inch lengths.

2. Sift together the flour and baking powder into a large bowl. Stir in the sugar. Lightly beat the eggs in a large jug, then beat in the milk and melted butter. Make a well in the centre of the dry ingredients and pour in the beaten liquid ingredients. Stir in the rhubarb, raisins and stem ginger until just combined; do not over-mix.

3. Spoon the mixture into the prepared muffin tin. Bake in the preheated oven for 15–20 minutes, until well risen, golden brown and firm to the touch.

4. Leave the muffins in the tin for 5 minutes, then serve warm or transfer to a wire rack and leave to cool.

COOK'S NOTE

Strip away any tough, fibrous or stringy ribs from the rhubarb stalks when preparing it.

Banana & Honey Muffins

MAKES 12

PREP TIME:
20 minutes

COOKING TIME:
20–25 minutes

nutritional information per muffin	207 kcals, 8g fat, 4g sat fat, 14g total sugars, 0.7g salt

These divine sweet muffins are flavoured with a delicious chopped banana and naturally sweetened with honey.

INGREDIENTS

- 280 g/10 oz self-raising flour
- 1 tsp baking powder
- ½ tsp bicarbonate of soda
- 1 tsp ground cinnamon
- pinch of salt
- 85 g/3 oz golden granulated sugar
- 85 g/3 oz butter, melted, plus extra for greasing (if using)
- 125 ml/4 fl oz milk
- 2 tbsp runny honey, plus extra for brushing
- 1 tsp vanilla extract
- 2 eggs
- 2 ripe bananas, mashed
- dried banana chips, to decorate

1. Preheat the oven to 180°C/350°F/Gas Mark 4. Grease a 12-cup muffin tin or line with 12 paper cases. Sift the flour, baking powder, bicarbonate of soda, cinnamon and salt into a large bowl. Add the sugar and stir to combine.

2. In a second bowl, beat the melted butter, milk, honey, vanilla extract, eggs and mashed banana together. Add to the flour mixture and stir lightly and thoroughly until just combined.

3. Spoon the mixture into the prepared muffin tin. Bake in the preheated oven for 20–25 minutes, or until well risen. Brush the top of each muffin with honey and top with a banana chip. Leave to cool in the tin for 5 minutes before transferring to a wire rack to cool or serve immediately.

4. Any remaining muffins will freeze for up to 2 months. When ready to use, defrost thoroughly and warm through in the oven.

1

2

2

SOMETHING DIFFERENT

You can use chopped banana chips instead of fresh banana, if that's all you have.

Home-made Jaffa Cakes

MAKES 12

PREP TIME:
45 minutes plus chilling

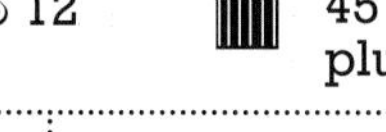
COOKING TIME:
10–12 minutes

nutritional information per cake	142 kcals, 6g fat, 3.5g sat fat, 16g total sugars, trace salt

A little fiddly to make but well worth the effort as these cakes will impress everyone!

INGREDIENTS

70 g/2½ oz orange jelly (6 cubes), finely chopped
100 ml/3½ fl oz boiling water
100 ml/3½ fl oz orange juice
2 eggs
50 g/1¾ oz caster sugar
50 g/1¾ oz plain flour
15 g/½ oz butter, melted and cooled, plus extra for greasing
150 g/5½ oz plain chocolate, broken into pieces

1. Place the chopped jelly and boiling water in a heatproof bowl and stir until the jelly has dissolved. Stir in the orange juice. Line a shallow 20-cm/8-inch square cake tin with clingfilm and pour in the jelly. Chill in the refrigerator for 2 hours until set.

2. Preheat the oven to 180°C/350°F/Gas Mark 4. Grease a 12-cup shallow bun tray.

3. Place the eggs and sugar in a large heatproof bowl set over a saucepan of simmering water. Using an electric whisk beat together until the mixture is thick and pale and leaves a trail on the surface when the whisk is lifted. Sift over the flour and fold in gently, then pour over the melted butter and fold in.

4. Spoon the mixture into the holes in the prepared bun tray. Bake in the preheated oven for 10–12 minutes until risen and golden. Cool for 2–3 minutes then loosen the cakes from the tray with a small palette knife and transfer to a wire rack to cool.

5. Place the chocolate in a heatproof bowl set over a pan of gently simmering water and leave until melted. Cool for 10–15 minutes.

6. Using a 4.5-cm/1¾-inch round cutter, stamp out 12 circles of jelly. Place one jelly circle on each sponge cake. Spoon the melted chocolate over the top and spread gently with the back of a spoon to completely cover the jelly and top of the cake. Leave in a cool place until the chocolate has set and then serve.

1
3
6

Scones

MAKES 12

PREP TIME:
20 minutes

COOKING TIME:
10–12 minutes

nutritional information per scone	190 kcals, 5g fat, 3g sat fat, 4g total sugars, 0.5g salt

The essential element for a traditional cream tea, these light and airy scones are best eaten on the day of making.

INGREDIENTS

450 g/1 lb plain flour, plus extra for dusting
½ tsp salt
2 tsp baking powder
55 g/2 oz butter
2 tbsp caster sugar
250 ml/9 fl oz milk
3 tbsp milk, for glazing
strawberry jam and clotted cream, to serve

1. Preheat the oven to 220°C/425°F/Gas Mark 7. Lightly flour or line a baking sheet with baking paper.

2. Sift the flour, salt and baking powder into a bowl. Rub in the butter until the mixture resembles breadcrumbs. Stir in the sugar. Make a well in the centre and pour in the milk. Stir in using a round-bladed knife and make a soft dough.

3. Turn the mixture onto a floured surface and lightly flatten the dough until it is of an even thickness, about 1 cm/½ inch. Don't be heavy handed, scones need a light touch.

4. Use a 6-cm/2½-inch pastry cutter to cut out the scones and place on the prepared baking sheet. Glaze with a little milk and bake in the preheated oven for 10–12 minutes, until golden and well risen. Cool on a wire rack and serve freshly baked, with strawberry jam and clotted cream.

2

2

4

COOK'S NOTE Jam or cream first - the choice is yours. Either way, be generous!

Spiced Teacakes

MAKES 8

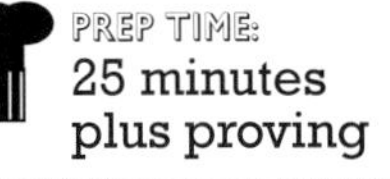

PREP TIME:
25 minutes
plus proving

COOKING TIME:
15–20 minutes

nutritional information per cake	323 kcals, 7g fat, 4g sat fat, 16g total sugars, 0.4g salt

These lightly fruited bread buns taste wonderful warm from the oven or toasted and buttered.

INGREDIENTS

- 450 g/1 lb strong plain flour, plus extra for dusting
- ½ tsp salt
- 2 tsp ground mixed spice
- 2 tsp fast action dried yeast
- 40 g/1½ oz caster sugar
- 115 g/4 oz mixed dried fruit
- 40 g/1½ oz butter, melted, plus extra for greasing
- 1 large egg, beaten
- 200 ml/7 fl oz warm milk, plus extra for brushing
- oil, for greasing

1. Sift the flour, salt and mixed spice into a large bowl. Stir in the dried yeast, sugar and mixed dried fruit and make a well in the centre.

2. Mix together the melted butter, egg and milk in a jug and pour into the well. Mix to a soft, slightly sticky dough. Turn onto a floured surface and knead for 5–6 minutes until the dough is smooth and elastic, adding a little more flour if the dough is too sticky.

3. Place the dough in a bowl, cover with lightly oiled clingfilm and leave in a warm place for about 1½ hours until doubled in size. Preheat the oven to 220°C/425°F/Gas Mark 7. Grease or line two baking sheets with baking paper.

4. Turn the dough onto a floured surface and knead again lightly for 1 minute. Divide the dough into eight pieces. Shape each piece into a ball then flatten with a rolling pin to a 9-cm/3½-inch circle. Place on the prepared baking sheets. Cover with clean tea towels and leave in a warm place for 30–40 minutes until risen and puffy.

5. Brush the teacakes lightly with milk. Bake in the preheated oven for 15–20 minutes until golden brown and the bases sound hollow when tapped. Transfer to a wire rack and serve warm or leave to cool completely.

2
3
4

Eccles Cakes

PREP TIME:
20 minutes

COOKING TIME:
15–20 minutes

nutritional information per cake	271 kcals, 13g fat, 7g sat fat, 22g total sugars, 0.4g salt

These classic crisp fruit pastries can be made in no time with ready-made puff pastry.

INGREDIENTS

40 g/1½ oz butter, plus extra for greasing
55 g/2 oz soft light brown sugar
225 g/8 oz currants
55 g/2 oz mixed peel
finely grated rind of ½ orange
½ tsp ground mixed spice
500 g/1 lb 2 oz ready-made puff pastry
flour, for dusting
2 tbsp milk
2 tbsp caster sugar

1. Preheat the oven to 220°C/425°F/Gas Mark 7. Lightly grease two baking sheets.

2. Place the butter in a small saucepan and heat gently until melted. Remove from the heat and stir in the brown sugar, currants, mixed peel, orange rind and mixed spice. Set aside.

3. Divide the pastry into 12 even-sized pieces. Roll each piece out on a lightly floured surface to a roughly-shaped circle about 12 cm/4½ inches in diameter. Heap a spoonful of the fruit filling in the centre of each pastry circle.

4. Lightly brush the pastry all around the filling with water. Gather together the pastry edges to completely enclose the filling and pinch them together tightly with your fingertips to seal. Turn each cake over and gently flatten with a rolling pin to a 10-cm/4-inch round. Place seam-side down on the prepared baking sheets.

5. With the tip of knife lightly score the top of each pastry four to five times. Brush with the milk and sprinkle over the caster sugar. Bake in the preheated oven for 15–20 minutes until crisp and golden brown. Transfer to a wire rack to cool.

2
3
4

Custard Tarts

PREP TIME: 25 minutes

nutritional information per tart	281 kcals, 20.5g fat, 11g sat fat, 9.5g total sugars, 0.3g salt

Quintessentially English, these delicious custard tarts have a long history in Britain and can be traced back to Medieval dinner tables.

INGREDIENTS

butter, for greasing
5 egg yolks, lightly beaten
100 g/3½ oz caster sugar
2 tsp cornflour
125 ml/4 fl oz milk
225 ml/8 fl oz double cream
5-cm/2-inch cinnamon stick
2 strips orange peel
½ teaspoon vanilla extract
375 g/13 oz ready-made puff pastry
freshly grated nutmeg, for sprinkling
flour, for dusting

1. Preheat the oven to 190°C/375°F/Gas Mark 5. Grease a 12-cup muffin tin. Combine the egg yolks and sugar in a mixing bowl. Stir in the cornflour and mix to a smooth paste, then whisk in the milk.

2. Heat the cream in a saucepan until just starting to simmer. Gradually whisk the hot cream into the egg mixture, then return the mixture to the pan. Add the cinnamon stick and orange peel. Cook over a medium heat, whisking constantly, for about 5 minutes, or until thickened. Immediately pour into a jug. Stir in the vanilla extract, then cover with clingfilm to prevent a skin forming and set aside.

3. Place the pastry on a board and trim to a rectangle measuring about 28 x 24 cm/11 x 9½ inches. Discard the trimmings or use in another recipe. Slice in half lengthways to make two rectangles, each measuring 28 x 12.5 cm/11 x 4¾ inches. Sprinkle one rectangle with freshly grated nutmeg. Place the other on top to make a sandwich, then roll up from the narrow end to make a log. Using a sharp knife, cut the log into twelve 1-cm/½-inch slices.

4. Roll out the slices on a floured surface to 5-cm/2-inch rounds. Place the rounds in the prepared muffin tin holes, lightly pressing down into the base and leaving a slightly thicker rim around the top edge.

5. Remove the cinnamon stick and orange peel from the custard and discard. Pour the custard into the pastry cases.

6. Bake in the preheated oven for 20 minutes, or until the crust and filling are golden brown. Leave to cool in the tin for 5 minutes, then transfer to a wire rack to cool completely.

1
3
4

Raspberry & Cream Meringues

MAKES 13

PREP TIME:
15 minutes
plus cooling

COOKING TIME:
1½ hours

nutritional information per meringue	194 kcals, 12.5g fat, 8g sat fat, 20g total sugars, 0.15g salt

These gorgeous meringues are just right for a romantic celebration or a special occasion.

INGREDIENTS

- 4 egg whites
- pinch of salt
- 125 g/4½ oz granulated sugar
- 125 g/4½ oz caster sugar
- 300 ml/10 fl oz double cream, lightly whipped, to serve
- raspberries, to serve

1. Preheat the oven to 120°C/250°F/Gas Mark ½. Line three baking sheets with baking paper.

2. Place the egg whites and a pinch of salt in a large clean bowl and, using an electric handheld whisk or balloon whisk, whisk until stiff. (You should be able to turn the bowl upside down without any movement from the whisked egg whites.)

3. Whisk in the granulated sugar, a little at a time; the meringue should begin to look glossy at this stage.

4. Sprinkle in the caster sugar, a little at a time, and continue whisking until all the sugar has been incorporated and the meringue is thick, white and forms peaks.

5. Transfer the meringue mixture to a piping bag fitted with a 2-cm/¾-inch star nozzle. Carefully pipe about 26 small whirls of the mixture on to the prepared baking sheets.

6. Bake in the preheated oven for 1½ hours, or until the meringues are pale golden in colour and can be easily lifted off the paper. Leave them to cool overnight in the turned-off oven.

7. Just before serving, sandwich the meringues together in pairs with the cream and arrange on a serving plate, with raspberries scattered around.

2
4
5

Lavender Shortbread

 SERVES 8

 PREP TIME: 20 minutes plus chilling

COOKING TIME: 30–35 minutes

nutritional information per serving	210 kcals, 12.5g fat, 8g sat fat, 7g total sugars, 0.2g salt

This Scottish favourite is enhanced with fragrant lavender flowers - perfect for afternoon tea.

INGREDIENTS

115 g/4 oz butter, softened, plus extra for greasing

55 g/2 oz lavender caster sugar, plus extra for sprinkling (see Cook's Note)

140 g/5 oz plain flour

25 g/1 oz cornflour

1. Preheat the oven to 160°C/325°F/Gas Mark 3. Lightly grease a baking sheet. Place the butter in a bowl. Sift over the caster sugar (reserving the lavender flowers left in the sieve) and beat together with a wooden spoon until light and fluffy.

2. Sift over the flour and cornflour and add the reserved lavender. Gradually work the flours into the creamed mixture to form a crumbly dough. Gather the dough together with your hands and knead lightly until smooth. Wrap the dough in clingfilm and chill in the refrigerator for 20 minutes.

3. Place the dough on the baking sheet and, using clean hands, press it out to an 18-cm/7-inch circle. Smooth the top by gently rolling a rolling pin over the mixture a couple of times. Crimp around the edge and mark into eight triangles with a sharp knife. Sprinkle with a little more lavender sugar. Chill in the refrigerator for at least 30 minutes until firm. Bake in the preheated oven for 30–35 minutes until just pale golden. Leave the shortbread on the sheet for 10 minutes, then transfer to a wire rack to cool completely.

1

2

3

COOK'S NOTE

To make lavender sugar, mix 900 g/2 lb caster sugar with 4 teaspoons of clean and dry lavender flowers. Store in an airtight jar for up to 6 months.

Chocolate Caramel Shortbread

MAKES 12

PREP TIME:
30 minutes
plus chilling

COOKING TIME:
20–25 minutes

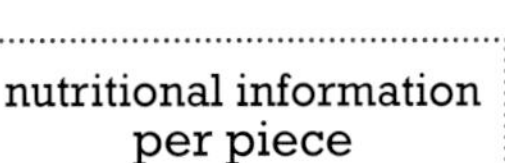

nutritional information per piece	500 kcals, 29g fat, 18g sat fat, 46g total sugars, 0.5g salt

Sometimes called millionaires' shortbread, these layered biscuit, caramel and chocolate squares are certainly pure indulgence!

INGREDIENTS

115 g/4 oz butter, plus extra for greasing
175 g/6 oz plain flour
55 g/2 oz golden caster sugar

filling & topping
175 g/6 oz butter
115 g/4 oz golden caster sugar
3 tbsp golden syrup
400 g/14 oz canned condensed milk
200 g/7 oz plain chocolate, broken into pieces

1. Preheat the oven to 180°C/350°F/Gas Mark 4. Grease and line a 23-cm/9-inch shallow square cake tin with baking paper.

2. Place the butter, flour and sugar in a food processor and process until it begins to bind together. Press the mixture into the prepared tin and smooth the top. Bake in the preheated oven for 20–25 minutes.

3. Meanwhile, make the filling. Place the butter, sugar, golden syrup and condensed milk in a saucepan and heat gently until the sugar has dissolved. Bring to the boil and simmer for 6–8 minutes, stirring constantly, until the mixture becomes very thick. Pour over the shortbread base and leave to chill in the refrigerator until firm.

4. To make the topping, place the chocolate in a heatproof bowl, set the bowl over a saucepan of gently simmering water and heat until melted, then spread over the caramel. Chill in the refrigerator until set. Cut the shortbread into 12 pieces with a sharp knife and serve.

2

3

4

COOK'S NOTE

It's vital to stir the caramel mixture continuously to prevent it sticking to the pan.

Butter Biscuits

MAKES 24

PREP TIME:
10 minutes
plus chilling

COOKING TIME:
12–15 minutes

nutritional information per biscuit	122 kcals, 8g fat, 4.5g sat fat, 4g total sugars, 0.2g salt

These melt-in-the-mouth, bite-sized biscuits are made with icing sugar, egg yolks, vanilla and lots of butter.

INGREDIENTS

- 250 g/9 oz plain flour, plus extra for dusting
- 100 g/3½ oz icing sugar, sifted
- pinch of salt
- 200 g/7 oz chilled butter, diced and frozen for 10 minutes
- 2 large egg yolks, beaten with ½ tsp vanilla extract
- 1 egg yolk, beaten with 1 tsp milk, to glaze

1. If you have time, put the food processor blade in the refrigerator to chill before you make the dough. Blend the flour, sugar and salt in a food processor. Add the butter and process until fine crumbs form. With the motor running, add the vanilla egg yolks through the feed tube and process until a soft dough forms. Do take care not to overwork the dough. Scrape the dough out of the food processor bowl onto a lightly floured work surface and divide into two portions. Quickly knead each portion into a ball, wrap in clingfilm and chill in the refrigerator for at least 30 minutes.

2. Meanwhile, line two baking sheets that will fit in your fridge with baking paper. Very lightly flour the work surface and a rolling pin. Take one dough ball out of the refrigerator and roll out until it is 5 mm/¼ inch thick. Use a floured 6-cm/2½-inch round cutter to cut out 12 biscuits, quickly re-rolling the trimmings. Brush any excess flour off the top of the biscuits and use a metal spatula to transfer them to one of the prepared baking sheets. Handle the dough as little as possible and, if it becomes soft and buttery at any point, return it to the refrigerator to chill. Place the baking sheet in the refrigerator while you roll out the remaining dough and cut out more biscuits. Chill all the biscuits for at least 30 minutes before baking.

3. Meanwhile, preheat the oven to 180°C/350°F/Gas Mark 4. Lightly brush the biscuits with the egg glaze and return them to the refrigerator while the oven heats. Bake in the preheated oven for 12–15 minutes, or until they are golden brown at the edges. Remove the baking sheets from the oven and leave the biscuits to stand for 5 minutes, then transfer to wire racks to cool completely.

2
3
3

Spicy Apple Bars

PREP TIME:
15 minutes

COOKING TIME:
45–55 minutes

nutritional information per bar	213 kcals, 12g fat, 6.5g sat fat, 13.5g total sugars, 0.15g salt

A lovely sweet treat, these crunchy bars are great for snacks and packed lunches.

INGREDIENTS

2 crisp eating apples, peeled, cored and diced
2 tbsp lemon juice
125 g/4½ oz unsalted butter, softened, plus extra for greasing
125 g/4½ oz golden caster sugar
1 tsp vanilla extract
2 eggs, beaten
150 g/5½ oz self-raising flour

topping
40 g/1½ oz almonds, chopped
40 g/1½ oz plain flour
40 g/1½ oz light muscovado sugar
½ tsp ground cinnamon
30 g/1 oz unsalted butter, melted

1. Preheat the oven to 180°C/350°F/Gas Mark 4. Grease a 28 x 18-cm/11 x 7-inch baking tin and line with baking paper. Sprinkle the apples with lemon juice.

2. Cream together the butter, sugar and vanilla extract until pale. Gradually add the eggs, beating thoroughly.

3. Sift over the flour and fold in evenly, then stir in the apples. Spread evenly in the prepared tin.

4. For the topping, mix all the ingredients to a crumbly texture, sprinkle over the cake and bake in the preheated oven for 45–55 minutes, until firm and golden. Cut into bars and serve cold or warm.

1
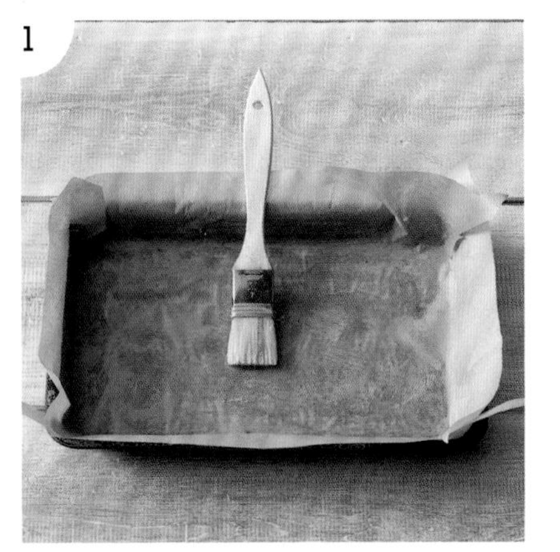

2

3

BE PREPARED

These tasty bars will keep for up to 1 week when stored within an airtight container.

Sugar Plums

MAKES 16

PREP TIME:
15 minutes plus chilling

COOKING TIME:
No cooking

nutritional information per piece	110 kcals, 4.5g fat, 0.5g sat fat, 12.5g total sugars, trace salt

These delightful bite-sized fruity sweets are perfect for serving with a cup of tea or spiced hot chocolate at Christmas.

INGREDIENTS

- 100 g/3½ oz blanched almonds
- 55 g/2 oz ready-to-eat dried apricots or figs, chopped
- 35 g/1¼ oz sultanas or raisins
- 35 g/1¼ oz dried cranberries
- 2 tbsp strawberry jam
- 2 tbsp soft light brown sugar
- 1 tsp ground mixed spice
- ½ tsp ground ginger
- ¼ tsp ground cardamom
- grated zest of 1 large orange
- 35 g/1¼ oz shelled pistachio nuts, finely chopped
- 100 g/3½ oz caster sugar
- 1 tsp ground cinnamon

1. Put the almonds into a food processor and process until finely ground. Remove one third of the almonds and set aside. Add the apricots, sultanas and cranberries to the food processor and pulse until finely chopped. Add the jam, brown sugar, mixed spice, ginger, cardamom and orange zest and pulse again until blended and a sticky paste forms. Stir in the nuts but do not pulse.

2. Divide the mixture into 16 equal portions and roll each portion into a ball, then set aside.

3. Place a sheet of baking paper on a work surface and sift over the caster sugar, cinnamon and reserved ground almonds. Add the sugarplum balls and roll them around until they are well coated. Place each sugar plum in a small paper case, then transfer to an airtight container and refrigerate for up to 2 weeks. Do take care not to stack the sugar plums on top of each other or they will flatten.

1

1

3

SOMETHING DIFFERENT
Instead of rolling the balls in icing sugar, dip into melted and cooled white chocolate.

Coconut Ice

PREP TIME:
15 minutes
plus setting

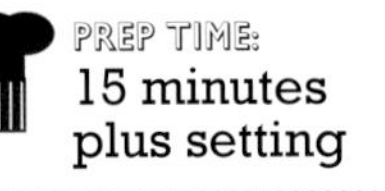

COOKING TIME:
No cooking

nutritional information per piece	90 kcals, 5g fat, 4g sat fat, 10.5g total sugars, trace salt

This is a colourful and tasty variation on a very classic British sweet, with a layer of chocolate-flavoured coconut ice. It is delicious served as petits four with coffee, but also makes a lovely gift.

INGREDIENTS

- oil, for greasing
- 400 g/14 oz canned condensed milk
- 1 tsp vanilla extract
- 300 g/10½ oz desiccated coconut
- 300 g/10½ oz icing sugar
- 3 tbsp cocoa powder, sifted
- few drops of red or pink food colouring (optional)

1. Grease the base of a shallow 18-cm/7-inch square cake tin and line with baking paper. Mix the condensed milk and vanilla extract together in a large bowl. Add the coconut and icing sugar. Mix together with a wooden spoon until the mixture becomes very stiff.

2. Transfer half of the mixture to another bowl. Add the cocoa powder and mix well until it is an even colour. Spread over the base of the prepared tin and press down with the back of a spoon.

3. If using food colouring, mix a few drops into the remaining bowl of mixture until evenly pink in colour. Spread over the chocolate layer and smooth the top. Leave to set overnight before turning out and cutting into squares.

1

2

3

BE PREPARED

You can make the coconut ice up to 2 weeks in advance and store in an airtight container.

Nut Fudge

 MAKES 80

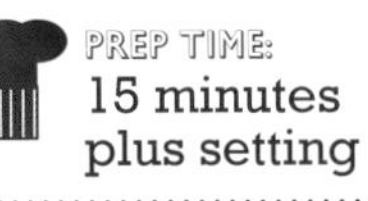 PREP TIME: 15 minutes plus setting

COOKING TIME: 15 minutes

nutritional information per piece	104 kcals, 4.5g fat, 2g sat fat, 16g total sugars, trace salt

Home-made fudge is a delicious treat and is surprisingly easy to make. Make sure you have a good heavy-based saucepan to prevent the boiling mixture from sticking and take care as the mixture will be extremely hot.

INGREDIENTS

- 300 ml/10 fl oz milk
- 1 kg/2 lb 4 oz golden granulated sugar
- 250 g/9 oz butter, plus extra for greasing
- 2 tbsp instant coffee granules
- 2 tbsp cocoa powder
- 2 tbsp golden syrup
- 400 g/14 oz canned condensed milk
- 115 g/4 oz shelled pecan nuts, chopped

1. Grease a 30 x 23 cm/12 x 9 inch Swiss roll tin. Place the milk, sugar and butter in a large saucepan. Stir over a gentle heat until the sugar has dissolved. Stir in the coffee granules, cocoa, golden syrup and condensed milk.

2. Bring to the boil and boil steadily, whisking constantly, for 10 minutes, or until a little of the mixture, dropped into a small bowl of cold water, forms a soft ball when rolled between the fingers.

3. Cool for 5 minutes, then beat vigorously with a wooden spoon until the mixture starts to thicken. Stir in the nuts. Continue beating until the mixture becomes thick, creamy and grainy. Quickly pour into the prepared tin and stand in a cool place to set. Cut the fudge into squares to serve.

1

2

3

COOK'S NOTE

To make the fudge easier to cut, mark into squares as the mixture is cooling.

Dinner

Prime Rib of Beef au Jus

 SERVES 8

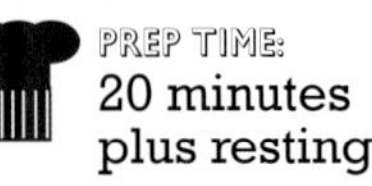 PREP TIME: 20 minutes plus resting

COOKING TIME: 2–2½ hours

nutritional information per serving	480 kcals, 24g fat, 12g sat fat, 0.5g total sugars, 1.4g salt

This really is the ultimate roast – a prime joint of tender beef cooked to perfection. Serve with roast potatoes and freshly cooked vegetables for the full Sunday lunch experience!

INGREDIENTS

2.7 kg/6 lb rib of beef
55 g/2 oz butter, softened
1½ tsp sea salt flakes
1 tbsp ground black pepper
2 tbsp flour
1 litre/1¾ pints beef stock
thyme sprigs, to garnish
roast potatoes and vegetables, to serve

1. Place the beef bone-side down in a deep-sided flameproof roasting tin. Rub the entire surface of the meat with butter, and coat evenly with the salt and black pepper.

2. Leave the beef to reach room temperature for 1 hour. Preheat the oven to 230°C/450°F/Gas Mark 8. Place the meat in the preheated oven and allow to roast uncovered for 20 minutes to sear the outside of the roast.

3. Reduce the heat to 160°C/325°F/Gas Mark 3 and roast for 15 minutes per 450 g/1 lb of meat for medium-rare (plus or minus 15 minutes for well done and rare respectively). Transfer the meat to a large platter and cover with foil. Allow to rest for 30 minutes before serving.

4. Pour off all but 2 tablespoons of the fat from the pan and place the roasting tin over a medium heat. Add the flour to the roasting pan and simmer, stirring with a wooden spoon for 1 minute to form a thick paste. Pour in a ladleful of beef stock, bring to the boil, stirring and scraping all the caramelized beef drippings from the bottom of the pan. Repeat with the remaining stock, a ladleful at a time. Simmer for 10 minutes.

5. Serve the beef with the 'jus' accompanied by roast potatoes and vegetables and garnished with thyme sprigs.

1
4
4

Home-made Fish Fingers

SERVES 8

PREP TIME:
20 minutes

COOKING TIME:
40–50 minutes

nutritional information per serving	224 kcals, 6g fat, 1g sat fat, 4g total sugars, 0.6g salt

These home-made fish fingers are fun for all the family - children love the simple flavours and grown ups love the nostalgia factor!

INGREDIENTS

280 g/10 oz thick cod fillets, skin and bones removed
flour, for dusting
1 tsp paprika
fresh breadcrumbs or fine cornmeal, for coating
1 egg, beaten
sunflower oil, for frying
salt and pepper
fresh or frozen peas, cooked, to serve

sweet potato wedges
450 g/1 lb sweet potatoes, scrubbed and cut into wedges
1 tbsp olive oil

1. To make the potato wedges, preheat the oven to 200°C/400°F/Gas Mark 6. Dry the sweet potato wedges on a clean tea towel. Place the oil in a roasting tin and heat for a few minutes in the oven. Arrange the potatoes in the tin and bake for 30–35 minutes, turning them halfway through, until tender and golden.

2. Meanwhile, cut the cod into strips about 2-cm/¾-inch wide. Put the flour onto a plate, add the paprika and season to taste. Put the breadcrumbs onto a second plate. Roll the cod strips in the seasoned flour until coated, shaking off any excess, then dip them in the beaten egg. Roll the cod strips in the breadcrumbs until evenly coated.

3. Heat enough oil to cover the base of a large, non-stick frying pan. Carefully arrange the fish fingers in the pan – you may have to cook them in batches – and fry them for 3–4 minutes on each side or until crisp and golden. Drain on kitchen paper before serving, if necessary. Serve the fish fingers with the sweet potato wedges and peas.

1

2

3

COOK'S NOTE

These home-made fish fingers are much tastier than their shop-bought equivalents and are quick and easy to make.

Roast Turkey

SERVES 8

PREP TIME: 20 minutes plus resting

COOKING TIME: 3½ hours

nutritional information per serving	256 kcals, 4.5g fat, 1.5g sat fat, 0.2g total sugars, 0.3g salt

Nothing beats roast turkey and all the trimmings on Christmas Day. For the best flavour, choose a fresh bird - free range if you can afford it!

INGREDIENTS

115 g/4 oz ready-made sausage stuffing (or see page 280)

1 turkey, weighing 5 kg/11 lb

40 g/1½ oz butter

bay leaves, sage leaves and chives, to garnish

to serve

bread sauce (see page 290)

roast potatoes

roast vegetables

1. Preheat the oven to 220°C/425°F/Gas Mark 7. Prepare the stuffing and spoon it into the neck cavity of the turkey and close the flap of skin with a skewer. Place the bird in a large roasting tin and rub it all over with the butter. Roast in the preheated oven for 1 hour, then lower the oven temperature to 180°C/350°F/Gas Mark 4 and roast for a further 2½ hours. You may need to pour off the fat from the roasting tin occasionally.

2. Check that the turkey is cooked by inserting a skewer or the point of a sharp knife into the thickest part of the thigh – if the juices run clear, it is ready. Transfer the bird to a carving board, cover loosely with foil and leave to rest.

3. Garnish the turkey with bay and sage leaves and chives. Carve and serve roughly 150 g/5½ oz of turkey per person, with the warm bread sauce, roast potatoes and vegetables.

1

1

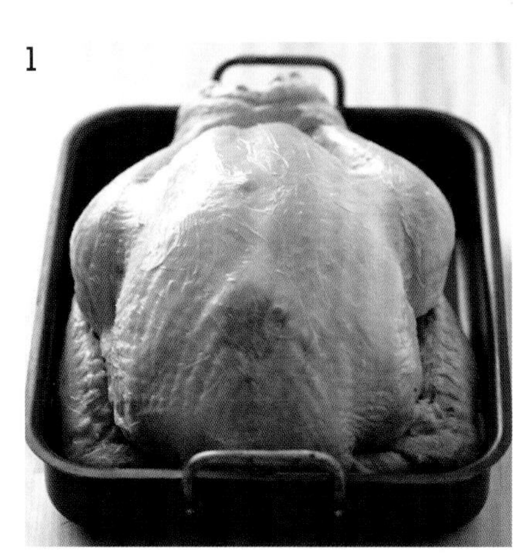

3

COOK'S NOTE

For extra flavour, place some fresh thyme sprigs in the main cavity of the turkey.

Roast Pheasant with Game Chips

SERVES 4

PREP TIME: 20 minutes plus resting

COOKING TIME: 1 hour

nutritional information per serving	747 kcals, 55g fat, 20g sat fat, 1g total sugars, 0.6g salt

A delicious roast for the colder months, pheasant has a good rich flavour and is traditionally served with crisp, fried slices of potato called game chips.

INGREDIENTS

100 g/3½ oz butter, slightly softened
1 tbsp chopped fresh thyme
1 tbsp chopped fresh parsley
2 oven-ready young pheasants
4 tbsp vegetable oil
125 ml/4 fl oz red wine
salt and pepper

game chips

650 g/1 lb 7 oz potatoes
sunflower oil, for frying

1. Preheat the oven to 190°C/375°F/Gas Mark 5. Put the butter in a small bowl and mix in the chopped herbs. Lift the skins off the pheasants and push the herb butter under the skins. Season to taste.

2. Pour the oil into a roasting tin, add the pheasants and roast in the preheated oven for 45 minutes, basting occasionally. Remove from the oven, pour over the wine, then return to the oven for 15 minutes, or until cooked through. Check the meat is cooked by inserting a knife between the legs and body, the juices should run clear.

3. To make the game chips, peel the potatoes and cut into thin slices. Immediately place in a bowl of cold water. Heat the oil in a deep fryer to 190°C/375°F, or until a cube of bread browns in 30 seconds. Drain the potato slices and pat dry with kitchen paper. Deep-fry, in batches, for 2–3 minutes, stirring, and remove with a slotted spoon. Drain on kitchen paper. Remove the pheasants from the oven, cover with foil and leave to rest for 15 minutes. Serve on a platter with game chips.

1

1

2

GOES WELL WITH

Serve with gravy made from the cooking juices and a spoonful of redcurrant jelly or onion gravy (see page 292).

Roast Sea Bass with Fennel & Orange

SERVES 2

PREP TIME:
20 minutes

COOKING TIME:
40 minutes

nutritional information per serving	650 kcals, 27g fat, 7g sat fat, 7g total sugars, 0.8 g salt

Sea bass has a lovely, delicate-flavoured white flesh, which is perfectly complemented by the orange and fennel in this dish.

INGREDIENTS

- 350 g/12 oz new potatoes, halved if large
- 2 tbsp olive oil
- 1 small orange
- 2 whole sea bass, about 450 g/1 lb each, cleaned, scaled, and heads and fins removed
- ½ fennel bulb, thinly sliced
- 1 tbsp roughly chopped fresh rosemary
- 15 g/½ oz butter, melted
- 2 garlic cloves, thinly sliced
- salt and pepper

1. Preheat the oven to 200°C/400°F/Gas Mark 6. Place the potatoes in a roasting tin that is large enough to hold everything in a single layer. Drizzle with 1 tablespoon of the oil, toss together and roast in the preheated oven for 20 minutes.

2. Meanwhile, pare the zest from the orange using a zester. Cut the orange into slices. Make three or four cuts in the plumpest part of each sea bass on both sides, cutting almost down to the bone. Season to taste with salt and pepper and place two or three orange slices inside the cavity of each.

3. Add the fennel and rosemary to the tin. Toss them with the potatoes and season to taste. Place the sea bass amongst the vegetables. Mix together the orange zest, melted butter, garlic and remaining oil. Spoon over the sea bass. Scatter over the remaining orange slices, then return the roasting tin to the oven for a further 20 minutes, until the fish is just cooked through and the vegetables are tender. Serve immediately.

2

3

3

SOMETHING DIFFERENT
Replace the fennel with roughly chopped celery or wedges of yellow pepper if preferred.

Crown of Roast Lamb

SERVES 6

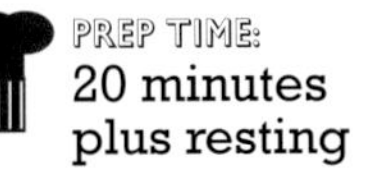
PREP TIME:
20 minutes
plus resting

COOKING TIME:
1¾–2¼ hours

nutritional information per serving	533 kcals, 26g fat, 9g sat fat, 12g total sugars, 0.4g salt

Often the traditional choice for Easter Day, this dish always makes an impressive centrepiece for any meal.

INGREDIENTS

1.6 kg/3 lb 8 oz crown of lamb
2 tbsp olive oil
salt and pepper

stuffing
100 g/3½ oz long-grain rice
2 tbsp vegetable oil
1 onion, finely chopped
2 celery sticks, finely chopped
2 garlic cloves, crushed
25 g/1 oz shelled pistachios
zest of 1 lemon, juice of ½ lemon
2 tbsp finely chopped mint
2 tbsp finely chopped parsley
100 g/3½ oz raisins

1. Calculate the cooking time of the lamb by allowing 25 minutes per 450 g/1 lb plus 25 minutes for medium, or 30 minutes per 450 g/1 lb plus 30 minutes for well done. Place the crown in a deep roasting tin, brush the outside with the oil and season with salt and pepper. Preheat the oven to 180°C/350°F/Gas Mark 4.

2. To make the stuffing, cook the rice until just al dente. Drain and cool. Heat the oil in a frying pan and sauté the onion and celery for 4–5 minutes. Add the garlic and cook for a further 1 minute until softened but not browned. Stir into the cooled rice, together with the pistachios, lemon zest and juice, herbs and raisins.

3. Fill the centre of the crown with the stuffing, cover the ends of the bones with foil to prevent burning, then cover the whole joint with foil. Roast for the calculated time, removing the foil for the last 10–15 minutes. At the end of the cooking time, remove from the oven, lift out of the tin, re-cover completely with foil and allow to rest for 20 minutes. Serve with the stuffing.

1

2

3

COOK'S NOTE
This dish is delicious when served with fresh mint sauce (see page 298).

Nut Roast

SERVES 4

PREP TIME:
30 minutes
plus cooling

COOKING TIME:
50 minutes

nutritional information per serving	650 kcals, 39g fat, 11g sat fat, 26g total sugars, 1.5g salt

Packed full of flavour, this nut roast is perfect for a vegetarian Sunday dinner.

INGREDIENTS

25 g/1 oz butter, plus extra for greasing
1 tbsp olive oil
1 red onion, chopped
200 g/7 oz cooked and peeled chestnuts, chopped
115 g/4 oz fresh white or wholemeal breadcrumbs
150 g/5½ oz Brazil nuts, coarsely ground
1 tbsp soy sauce
2 tbsp chopped fresh flat-leaf parsley
2 tbsp chopped fresh sage
2 eggs, beaten
salt and pepper

cranberry glaze

200 ml/7 fl oz orange juice
1 tbsp white wine vinegar
40 g/1½ oz soft light brown sugar
2 tbsp redcurrant jelly
pinch of ground cloves
175 g/6 oz fresh cranberries

1. Preheat the oven to 180°C/350°F/Gas Mark 4. Grease a 450-g/1-lb loaf tin and line with baking paper.

2. Heat the butter and oil in a large deep frying pan and fry the chopped onion for 7–8 minutes until softened but not brown. Stir in the chopped chestnuts and cook for a further 4–5 minutes. Remove the pan from the heat and stir in the breadcrumbs, nuts, soy sauce and herbs. Cool for 20 minutes.

3. Stir in the beaten eggs and season well with salt and pepper. Pack the nut mixture into the prepared loaf tin and level the surface. Top with a strip of baking paper and cover tightly with foil. Place the loaf tin on a baking sheet and bake in the preheated oven for 50 minutes.

4. To make the cranberry glaze, place the orange juice, vinegar, sugar, redcurrant jelly and ground cloves in a saucepan. Heat gently until the sugar and jelly have dissolved then simmer for 8–10 minutes until syrupy. Stir in the cranberries and simmer for a further 3–4 minutes, or until they are just softened. Cool for 5 minutes.

5. To serve, turn the nut roast out onto a serving platter. Spoon some of the cranberry glaze over the top of the nut roast and transfer the rest to a small dish. Serve immediately.

2
3
4

Poached Salmon

SERVES 6

PREP TIME:
15 minutes
plus cooling

COOKING TIME:
2–8 minutes

nutritional information per 100g salmon	180 kcals, 11g fat, 2g sat fat, 0g total sugars, 0.5g salt

A whole poached salmon is an excellent choice for a summer dinner - it's easy to cook and is delicious served hot or cold.

INGREDIENTS

- 1 whole salmon (head on), about 2.7 kg/6 lb to 3.6 kg/8 lb prepared weight
- 3 tbsp salt
- 3 bay leaves
- 10 black peppercorns
- 1 onion, sliced
- 1 lemon, sliced
- lemon wedges, to serve

1. Wipe the salmon thoroughly inside and out with kitchen paper, then use the back of a cook's knife to remove any scales that might still be on the skin. Remove the fins with scissors and trim the tail. Some prefer to cut off the head but it is traditionally prepared with it on.

2. Place the salmon on the two-handled rack that comes with a fish kettle, then place it in the kettle. Fill the kettle with enough cold water to cover the salmon adequately. Sprinkle over the salt, bay leaves and peppercorns and scatter in the onion and lemon slices.

3. Place the kettle over a low heat, over two burners, and bring just to the boil very slowly. Cover and simmer very gently. To serve cold, simmer for 2 minutes only, remove from the heat and leave to cool in the liquor for about 2 hours with the lid on. To serve hot, simmer for 6–8 minutes and leave to stand in the hot water for 15 minutes before removing. Remove the fish from the kettle, skin and serve with lemon wedges for squeezing over.

1

2

3

GOES WELL WITH

Make a quick sauce by stirring fresh chopped mixed herbs and lemon juice into mayonnaise.

Glazed Gammon in Cider

SERVES 6

PREP TIME:
15 minutes

COOKING TIME:
4¼–4½ hours

nutritional information per 100g gammon	200 kcals, 11.5g fat, 4g sat fat, 2g total sugars, 2.8g salt

Gammon is the meat from the hind legs of a pig that has been cured in the same way as bacon. This dish makes a delicious change for a special evening meal.

INGREDIENTS

4 kg/9 lb gammon
1 apple, cored and chopped
1 onion, chopped
300 ml/10 fl oz cider
6 black peppercorns
1 bouquet garni
1 bay leaf
about 50 cloves
4 tbsp demerara sugar

1. Put the gammon in a large saucepan and add enough cold water to cover. Bring to the boil and skim off any foam that rises to the surface. Reduce the heat and simmer for 30 minutes.

2. Drain the gammon and return to the saucepan. Add the apple, onion, cider, peppercorns, bouquet garni, bay leaf and a few of the cloves. Pour in enough fresh water to cover and bring back to the boil. Cover and simmer for 3 hours 20 minutes.

3. Preheat the oven to 200°C/400°F/Gas Mark 6. Take the saucepan off the heat and set aside to cool slightly. Remove the gammon from the cooking liquid and, while it is still warm, loosen the rind with a sharp knife, then peel it off and discard.

4. Score the fat into diamond shapes and stud with the remaining cloves. Place the gammon on a rack in a roasting tin and sprinkle with the sugar. Roast in the preheated oven, basting occasionally with the cooking liquid, for 20 minutes. To check it is cooked, insert a skewer into the centre of the meat – the juices should run clear with no traces of pink and the meat should be cooked through, not pink. Serve hot or cold.

1
2
4

Lancashire Hot Pot

SERVES 6

PREP TIME:
30 minutes

COOKING TIME:
2½ hours

nutritional information per serving	462 kcals, 20g fat, 10g sat fat, 4g total sugars, 0.8g salt

Sometimes the simplest and cheapest ingredients make the most delicious meals, as in the case of this classic meat and potato hot pot.

INGREDIENTS

- 900 g/2 lb best end lamb chops
- 3 lambs' kidneys, cored and quartered
- 55 g/2 oz butter
- 900 g/2 lb floury potatoes, such as King Edward or Maris Piper, thinly sliced
- 3 onions, halved and finely sliced
- 2 tsp fresh thyme leaves
- 1 tsp finely chopped fresh rosemary
- 600 ml/1 pint chicken stock
- salt and pepper

1. Preheat the oven to 160°C/325°F/Gas Mark 3.

2. Trim the chops of any excess fat and place in a bowl. Add the kidneys to the bowl and season with salt and pepper to taste.

3. Grease a large, shallow ovenproof dish or deep roasting tin with half the butter and arrange a layer of potatoes in the bottom. Layer up the onions and meat, seasoning with salt and pepper to taste and sprinkling in the herbs between each layer. Finish with a neat layer of overlapping potatoes.

4. Pour in most of the stock so that it covers the meat. Melt the remaining butter and brush the top of the potato with it. Reserve any remaining butter. Cover with foil and cook in the preheated oven for 2 hours. Uncover the hotpot and brush the potatoes again with the melted butter. Return the hotpot to the oven and cook for a further 30 minutes, or until the potatoes are crisp and brown. Serve immediately.

2

3

3

COOK'S NOTE

Use a food processor with the slicing blade fitted to slice the potatoes thinly and evenly.

Chicken Kiev

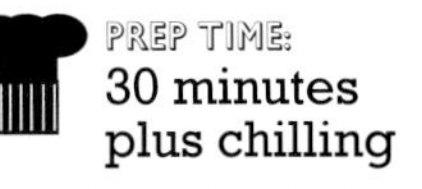

COOKING TIME: 8–10 minutes

nutritional information per serving	851 kcals, 47g fat, 19g sat fat, 1.5g total sugars, 1.7g salt

Another imported recipe that has become a British favourite, Chicken Kiev reached the height of its popularity during the 1970s and 80s. A good home-made version is still a tasty treat and this recipe fits the bill perfectly.

INGREDIENTS

- 115 g/4 oz butter, softened
- 3–4 garlic cloves, very finely chopped
- 1 tbsp chopped fresh parsley
- 1 tbsp snipped fresh chives
- juice and finely grated rind of ½ lemon
- 8 skinless, boneless chicken breasts, about 115 g/4 oz each
- 55 g/2 oz plain flour
- 2 eggs, lightly beaten
- 175 g/6 oz dry breadcrumbs
- groundnut or sunflower oil, for deep-frying
- salt and pepper
- green vegetables, to serve

1. Beat the butter in a bowl with the garlic, herbs, and lemon juice and rind. Season to taste with salt and pepper. Divide into eight pieces, then shape into cylinders. Wrap in foil and chill in the refrigerator until firm.

2. Place each chicken breast between two sheets of clingfilm. Pound gently with a meat mallet or rolling pin to flatten the chicken to an even thickness. Place a butter cylinder on each chicken piece and roll up. Secure with cocktail sticks.

3. Place the flour, eggs and breadcrumbs in separate shallow dishes. Dip the rolls into the flour, then the egg and, finally, the breadcrumbs. Chill in the refrigerator for 1 hour.

4. Heat enough oil for deep-frying in a saucepan or deep-fat fryer to 180–190°C/350–375°F, or until a cube of bread browns in 30 seconds. Deep-fry the chicken, in batches, for 8–10 minutes, or until cooked through and golden brown. Drain on kitchen paper. Serve immediately with green vegetables.

1
2
3

Toad in the Hole with Beer Batter

 SERVES 4

 PREP TIME: 15 minutes

COOKING TIME: 40 minutes

nutritional information per serving	690 kcals, 44g fat, 14g sat fat, 5g total sugars, 4.3g salt

A grown-up version of this low-cost family favourite with bacon, beer and fresh herbs.

INGREDIENTS

8 rashers streaky bacon
8 thick pork sausages
175 g/6 oz plain flour
pinch of salt
2 large eggs
150 ml/5 fl oz milk
150 ml/5 fl oz beer
1 tbsp chopped fresh thyme
2 tbsp sunflower oil
onion gravy, to serve (see page 292)

1. Preheat the oven to 220°C/425°F/Gas Mark 7. Wrap a bacon rasher around each sausage and place in a flameproof roasting tin (the tin will need to be approximately 30 cm x 23 cm/12 inches x 9 inches). Bake in the preheated oven for 10 minutes.

2. Place the flour and salt in a bowl. Make a well in the centre and add the eggs, then gradually beat in the milk, followed by the beer, to make a smooth batter. Stir in the thyme. Pour into a jug and set aside.

3. Pour away any watery juices from the roasting tin. Rearrange the sausages, add the oil and heat on the hob until smoking hot. Quickly pour the batter over the sausages and bake in the preheated oven for 25–30 minutes until risen, crisp and golden brown. Serve with gravy.

COOK'S NOTE

To avoid the just-risen batter deflating before it firms up, don't be tempted to open the oven door until the dish has been cooking for at least 20 minutes.

Shepherd's Pie

SERVES 6

PREP TIME:
30 minutes

COOKING TIME:
1¼–1½ hours

nutritional information per serving	442 kcals, 26g fat, 13g sat fat, 3g total sugars, 0.5g salt

A hearty and warming family favourite made with savoury minced lamb and topped with creamy mashed potato.

INGREDIENTS

1 tbsp olive oil
2 onions, finely chopped
2 garlic cloves, finely chopped
675 g/1 lb 8 oz good quality minced lamb
2 carrots, finely chopped
1 tbsp plain flour
225 ml/8 fl oz beef or chicken stock
125 ml/4 fl oz red wine
Worcestershire sauce (optional)
salt and pepper

mashed potato

675 g/1 lb 8 oz floury potatoes, such as King Edward, Maris Piper or Desirée, cut into chunks
55 g/2 oz butter
2 tbsp single cream or milk
salt and pepper

1. Preheat the oven to 180°C/350°F/Gas Mark 4.

2. Heat the oil in a large saucepan and fry the onion until softened, then add the garlic and stir well. Raise the heat and add the meat. Cook quickly to brown the meat all over, stirring continually. Add the carrots and season with salt and pepper to taste. Stir in the flour and add the stock and wine. Stir well and heat until simmering and thickened.

3. Place the meat mixture in a covered casserole and cook in the oven for about 1 hour. Check the consistency from time to time and add a little more stock or wine if required. The meat mixture should be quite thick but not dry. Season to taste with salt. Add a little Worcestershire sauce, if desired.

4. While the meat is cooking, make the mashed potato. Cook the potatoes in a large saucepan of lightly salted boiling water for 15–20 minutes. Drain and mash with a potato masher until smooth. Add the butter and cream and season with salt and pepper to taste. Spoon the lamb mixture into an ovenproof serving dish and spread or pipe the potato on top.

5. Increase the oven temperature to 200°C/400°F/Gas Mark 6 and cook the pie for a further 15–20 minutes at the top of the oven until golden brown. Remove from the oven and place under a medium grill until the topping is crisp and brown. Serve immediately.

2
4
4

Chicken Tikka Masala

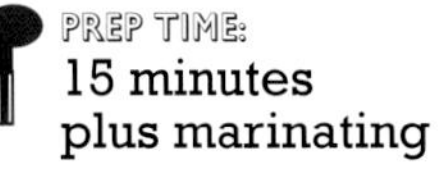

COOKING TIME:
35–40 minutes

nutritional information per serving	418 kcals, 22g fat, 8.5g sat fat, 12.5g total sugars, 1.6g salt

This mildly spiced Anglo-Indian curry is probably one of the most popular dishes on pub and restaurant menus.

INGREDIENTS

- 600 g/1 lb 5 oz skinless, boneless chicken breasts, cut into chunks
- 150 ml/5 fl oz natural yogurt
- 6 tbsp tikka paste
- 1 tsp brown sugar
- 1 tbsp sunflower oil
- 25 g/1 oz butter
- 1 large onion, chopped
- 400 g/14 oz canned chopped tomatoes
- 1 tbsp tomato purée
- 150 ml/5 fl oz water
- 125 ml/4 fl oz single cream
- 1–2 tbsp mango chutney
- handful of fresh coriander leaves, roughly chopped
- rice or naan bread, to serve

1. Mix the chicken, yogurt, 2 tablespoons of the tikka paste and the sugar together. Leave to marinate for at least 30 minutes or preferably overnight in the refrigerator.

2. Heat the oil and butter in a large frying pan. Add the onion and fry over a medium-low heat for 15 minutes, or until softened and golden brown. Preheat the grill to high.

3. Add the remaining tikka paste to the onions. Cook for 2 minutes, stirring constantly. Then stir in the chopped tomatoes, tomato purée and water to the pan. Simmer gently for 15 minutes.

4. Thread the chicken onto metal or pre-soaked wooden skewers and grill, close to the heat, for 15–20 minutes, turning halfway through, or until cooked through and charred in places. Stir the cream and chutney into the sauce, adding a little more water if it has become too thick and heat through for 1–2 minutes. Slide the hot chicken off the skewers using a fork and gently stir into the sauce. Sprinkle with the chopped fresh coriander and serve with rice or naan bread.

1

3

4

SOMETHING DIFFERENT

For a spicier curry, add one deseeded and finely chopped green chilli with the tikka paste at step 3.

Beef Wellington

SERVES 6

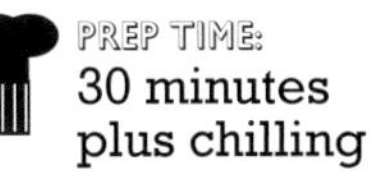
PREP TIME:
30 minutes plus chilling

COOKING TIME:
50 minutes

nutritional information per serving	867 kcals, 55.5g fat, 24g sat fat, 1.5g total sugars, 1.6g salt

Named after the Duke of Wellington in 1851, this sumptuous beef fillet wrapped in puff pastry makes an impressive main course for a special occasion.

INGREDIENTS

2 tbsp olive or vegetable oil
1.5 kg/3 lb 5 oz beef fillet, cut from the middle of the fillet, trimmed of fat and sinew
55 g/2 oz butter
150 g/5½ oz mushrooms, chopped
2 garlic cloves, crushed
150 g/5½ oz smooth liver pâté
few drops of truffle oil (optional)
1 tbsp finely chopped fresh parsley
2 tsp English mustard
500 g/1 lb 2 oz puff pastry
1 egg, lightly beaten
salt and pepper
roasted root vegetables, to serve

1. Place a large frying pan over a high heat and add the olive oil. Rub salt and pepper to taste into the beef and sear very quickly all over in the pan. (This method gives a rare version. If you want it less rare, roast it at 220°C/425°F/Gas Mark 7 for 20 minutes at this stage.) Set aside to cool.

2. Heat the butter in a frying pan over a medium heat, add the mushrooms and fry for 5 minutes. Reduce the heat, add the garlic and fry for another 5 minutes. Put the mushrooms and garlic in a bowl, add the pâté, truffle oil, if using, and parsley, and beat with a fork. Leave to cool.

3. Rub the mustard into the seared beef fillet. Roll out the pastry into a rectangle large enough to wrap the whole fillet with some to spare. Spread the mushroom paste in the middle of the pastry, leaving a 5-cm/2-inch gap between the paste and the edge of the pastry, and lay the beef on top. Brush the edges of the pastry with beaten egg and fold it over, edges overlapping, and across the meat to completely enclose it.

4. Preheat the oven to 220°C/425°F/Gas Mark 7. Place the wrapped beef in a roasting tin with the joint underneath and brush with beaten egg. Leave to chill in the refrigerator for 15 minutes, then transfer to the preheated oven and bake for 50 minutes. Check after 30 minutes – if the pastry looks golden brown, cover it in foil to prevent it burning.

5. Serve immediately with roasted root vegetables.

1
2
3

Pork Chops with Apple Sauce

SERVES 4

PREP TIME:
30 minutes

COOKING TIME:
10 minutes

nutritional information per serving	384 kcals, 15g fat, 4.5g sat fat, 24g total sugars, 0.3g salt

A lovely simple supper that's full of flavour – juicy pork chops roasted until tender and served with the perfect accompaniment of tart apple sauce.

INGREDIENTS

- 4 pork rib chops on the bone, each about 3 cm/1¼ inches thick, at room temperature
- 1½ tbsp sunflower oil or rapeseed oil
- salt and pepper

chunky apple sauce

- 450 g/1 lb cooking apples, such as Bramley, peeled, cored and diced
- 4 tbsp caster sugar, plus extra if needed
- finely grated zest of ½ lemon
- ½ tbsp lemon juice, plus extra if needed
- 4 tbsp water
- ¼ tsp ground cinnamon
- knob of butter

1. Preheat the oven to 200°C/400°F/Gas Mark 6.

2. For the apple sauce, put the apples, sugar, lemon zest, lemon juice and water into a heavy-based saucepan over a high heat and bring to the boil, stirring to dissolve the sugar. Reduce the heat to low, cover and simmer for 15–20 minutes, until the apples are tender and fall apart when you mash them against the side of the pan. Stir in the cinnamon and butter and beat the apples until they are as smooth or chunky as you like. Stir in extra sugar or lemon juice, to taste. Remove the pan from the heat, cover and keep the apple sauce warm.

3. Meanwhile, pat the chops dry and season to taste with salt and pepper. Heat the oil in a large ovenproof frying pan over a medium-high heat. Add the chops and fry for 3 minutes on each side to brown.

4. Transfer the pan to the oven and roast the chops for 7–9 minutes until cooked through and the juices run clear when you cut the chops. Remove the pan from the oven, cover with foil and leave to stand for 3 minutes. Gently reheat the apple sauce, if necessary.

5. Transfer the chops to warmed plates and spoon over the pan juices. Serve immediately, accompanied by the apple sauce.

2
2
3

Steak with Peppercorn Sauce & Sweet Potato Chips

PREP TIME: 15 minutes

COOKING TIME: 25–30 minutes

nutritional information per serving	824 kcals, 40g fat, 15g sat fat, 19g total sugars, 0.7g salt

Rustle up a restaurant-style meal at home with this easy-to-follow recipe.

INGREDIENTS

sweet potato chips

650 g/1 lb 7 oz sweet potatoes, peeled

2 tbsp olive oil

sea salt and pepper

steak

2 sirloin steaks (approximately 2 cm/¾ inch thick), at room temperature

1 tbsp olive oil

salt and pepper

peppercorn sauce

1 tbsp brandy

5 tbsp whipping cream

1½ tsp green peppercorns in brine, rinsed, drained and lightly crushed

1 small garlic clove, crushed

1 tsp Dijon mustard

1. To make the sweet potato chips, preheat the oven to 220°C/425°F/ Gas Mark 7. Trim the sweet potatoes and cut into 1-cm/½-inch slices and then into chips. Place on a baking sheet, drizzle with the olive oil and season with salt and pepper.

2. Mix well then spread out, slightly spaced apart. Bake in the preheated oven for 15 minutes until golden brown underneath, then flip over and cook for a further 10–15 minutes on the other side.

3. Start cooking the steaks and peppercorn sauce once the chips have been turned over. Preheat a heavy-based frying pan until smoking hot. Brush the steaks lightly with the oil and season.

4. Holding the steaks together, press the fatty edges onto the pan until well browned, then lay them flat and cook for about 1½ minutes on each side for rare steaks, or until cooked according to taste. Remove from the pan and keep warm.

5. Add the brandy to the frying pan, take off the heat and set alight. When the flames die down, stir in the cream, peppercorns, garlic and mustard. Heat for a few seconds until simmering and slightly thickened, then pour over the steaks. Serve immediately with the sweet potato chips.

2
4
5

Fisherman's Pie

PREP TIME:
20 minutes

COOKING TIME:
25–30 minutes

nutritional information per serving	531 kcals, 27g fat, 16g sat fat, 1.5g total sugars, 0.9g salt

Flaked fish and prawns in a creamy herb and wine sauce are topped with a thick layer of mashed potato - it's fish pie heaven!

INGREDIENTS

- 900 g/2 lb white fish fillets, such as plaice, skinned
- 150 ml/5 fl oz dry white wine
- 1 tbsp chopped fresh parsley, tarragon or dill
- 100 g/3½ oz butter, plus extra for greasing
- 175 g/6 oz small mushrooms, sliced
- 175 g/6 oz cooked, peeled prawns
- 40 g/1½ oz plain flour
- 125 ml/4 fl oz double cream
- 900 g/2 lb floury potatoes, such as King Edward, Maris Piper or Desirée, cut into chunks
- salt and pepper

1. Preheat the oven to 180°C/350°F/Gas Mark 4. Grease a 1.7-litre/3-pint baking dish. Fold the fish fillets in half and place in the dish. Season well with salt and pepper, pour over the wine and scatter over the herbs. Cover with foil and bake for 15 minutes until the fish starts to flake. Strain off the liquid and reserve for the sauce. Increase the oven temperature to 220°C/425°F/Gas Mark 7.

2. Heat 15 g/½ oz of the butter in a frying pan and sauté the mushrooms. Spoon the mushrooms over the fish and scatter over the prawns.

3. Add 55 g/2 oz of the butter to a saucepan, heat and stir in the flour. Cook for a few minutes without browning, remove from the heat, then add the reserved cooking liquid gradually, stirring well between each addition.

4. Return to the heat and gently bring to the boil, still stirring to ensure a smooth sauce. Add the cream and season to taste with salt and pepper. Pour over the fish in the dish and smooth over the surface.

5. Make the mashed potato by cooking the potatoes in boiling salted water for 15–20 minutes. Drain well and mash with a potato masher until smooth. Season to taste with salt and pepper and add the remaining butter.

6. Pile or pipe the potato onto the fish and sauce and bake in the oven for 10–15 minutes until golden brown.

1
4
6

Sausages & Mash with Onion Gravy

SERVES 4

PREP TIME:
15 minutes

COOKING TIME:
45 minutes

nutritional information per serving	784 kcals, 51g fat, 25g sat fat, 11g total sugars, 2.6g salt

This is a real British pub favourite - chunky fried sausages served on a bed of the creamiest mashed potato and smothered in rich onion gravy.

INGREDIENTS

1 tbsp olive oil

8 good quality sausages

onion gravy

3 onions, cut in half and thinly sliced

70 g/2½ oz butter

125 ml/4 fl oz Marsala or port

125 ml/4 fl oz vegetable stock

salt and pepper

mashed potato

900 g/2 lb floury potatoes, such as King Edward, Maris Piper or Desirée, cut into chunks

55 g/2 oz butter

3 tbsp hot milk

2 tbsp chopped fresh parsley

salt and pepper

1. Place a frying pan over a low heat with the oil and add the sausages. Cover the pan and cook for 25–30 minutes, turning the sausages from time to time, until browned all over.

2. Meanwhile, prepare the onion gravy by placing the onions in a large casserole with the butter and frying over a low heat until soft, stirring continuously. Continue to cook for around 30 minutes, or until the onions are brown and have started to caramelize.

3. Pour in the Marsala and stock and continue to bubble away until the onion gravy is really thick. Season to taste with salt and pepper.

4. To make the mashed potato, cook the potatoes in a large saucepan of lightly salted boiling water for 15–20 minutes. Drain well and mash with a potato masher until smooth. Season with salt and pepper to taste, add the butter, milk and parsley and stir well.

5. Serve the sausages immediately with the mashed potato and the onion gravy spooned over the top.

2
2
4

Hearty Beef Stew

SERVES 4

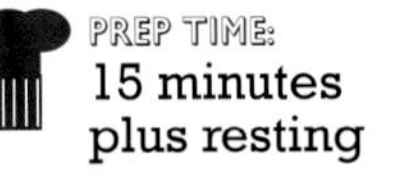
PREP TIME:
15 minutes
plus resting

COOKING TIME:
2¼–2½ hours

nutritional information per serving	755 kcals, 25g fat, 9g sat fat, 11g total sugars, 1.1g salt

Packed full of goodness, this classic beef stew is made by slowly cooking lean braising steak, onions and vegetables in a flavoursome stock with herbs and garlic - creating the perfect winter warming supper!

INGREDIENTS

- 1.3 kg/3 lb boneless braising steak, cut into 5-cm/2-inch pieces
- 2 tbsp vegetable oil
- 2 onions, cut into 2.5-cm/1-inch pieces
- 3 tbsp plain flour
- 3 garlic cloves, finely chopped
- 1 litre/1¾ pints beef stock
- 3 carrots, cut into 2.5-cm/1-inch lengths
- 2 celery sticks, cut into 2.5-cm/1-inch lengths
- 1 tbsp tomato ketchup
- 1 bay leaf
- ¼ tsp dried thyme
- ¼ tsp dried rosemary
- 900 g/2 lb potatoes, such as Maris Piper, cut into large chunks
- salt and pepper

1. Season the steak very generously with salt and pepper. Heat the oil in a large flameproof casserole over a high heat. When the oil begins to smoke slightly, add the steak, in batches, if necessary, and cook, stirring frequently, for 5–8 minutes, until well browned. Using a slotted spoon, transfer to a bowl.

2. Reduce the heat to medium, add the onions to the casserole and cook, stirring occasionally, for 5 minutes, until translucent. Stir in the flour and cook, stirring constantly, for 2 minutes. Add the garlic and cook for 1 minute. Whisk in 225 ml/8 fl oz of the stock and cook, scraping up all the sediment from the base of the casserole, then stir in the remaining stock and add the carrots, celery, tomato ketchup, bay leaf, thyme, rosemary and 1 teaspoon of salt. Return the steak to the casserole.

3. Bring back to a gentle simmer, cover and cook over a low heat for 1 hour. Add the potatoes, re-cover the casserole and simmer for a further 30 minutes. Remove the lid, increase the heat to medium and cook, stirring occasionally, for a further 30 minutes, or until the meat and vegetables are tender.

4. If the stew becomes too thick, add a little more stock or water and adjust the seasoning, if necessary. Leave to rest for 15 minutes before serving.

1
2
3

Fish & Chips with Mushy Peas

SERVES 4

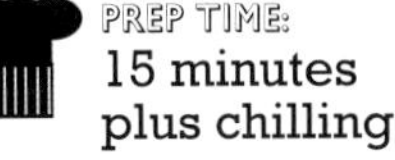
PREP TIME:
15 minutes plus chilling

COOKING TIME:
25–30 minutes

nutritional information per serving	913 kcals, 33g fat, 8g sat fat, 5g total sugars, 1.4g salt

Forget the takeaway and cook up this classic combination at home. Prepare everything before you start and check the oil is at the correct temperature for the best results.

INGREDIENTS

batter

- 225 g/8 oz self-raising flour, plus extra for dusting
- ½ tsp salt
- 300 ml/10 fl oz cold lager

mushy peas

- 350 g/12 oz frozen peas
- 30 g/1 oz butter
- 2 tbsp single cream
- salt and pepper

- vegetable oil, for deep-frying
- 6 large floury potatoes, such as King Edward, Maris Piper or Desirée, cut into chips
- 4 thick cod fillets, about 175 g/6 oz each
- salt and pepper

1. Sift the flour into a bowl with the salt and whisk in most of the lager. Check the consistency and add the remaining lager; it should be thick, like double cream. Chill in the refrigerator for half an hour.

2. Cook the peas in lightly salted boiling water for 3 minutes. Drain and mash to a thick purée, add the butter and cream and season with salt and pepper to taste. Set aside and keep warm.

3. Heat the oil to 120°C/250°F in a thermostatically controlled deep fat fryer or a large saucepan using a thermometer. Preheat the oven to 150°C/300°F/Gas Mark 2. Fry the chips for about 8–10 minutes until softened but not coloured. Remove from the oil, drain on kitchen paper and place in a dish in the warm oven. Increase the temperature of the oil to 180°C/350°F.

4. Season the fish with salt and pepper to taste and dust lightly with a little flour. Dip one fillet in the batter and coat thickly.

5. Carefully place in the hot oil and repeat with the other fillets (you may need to cook two at a time if your pan is small). Cook for 8–10 minutes, turning them over halfway through. Remove the fish from the oil, drain and keep warm.

6. Reheat the oil to 180°C/350°F and recook the chips for a further 2–3 minutes until golden brown. Drain and season with salt and pepper to taste. Serve with the fish and mushy peas.

1
2
4

Lamb's Liver with Bacon, Onions & Sage

PREP TIME:
20 minutes

COOKING TIME:
40 minutes

nutritional information per serving	530 kcals, 35g fat, 13.5g sat fat, 7g total sugars, 1.6g salt

The secret of this dish is to be very patient. Cook the onions slowly, then cook the liver as quickly as you can!

INGREDIENTS

55 g/2 oz butter
450 g/1 lb onions, thinly sliced
550 g/1 lb 4 oz sliced lamb's liver
2 plump unpeeled garlic cloves
6 rashers rindless smoked streaky bacon
1½–2 tbsp olive oil
12–14 small sage leaves
4 tsp plain flour
450 ml/16 fl oz vegetable stock
5 tbsp dry sherry
salt and pepper
mashed potatoes or soft polenta, to serve

1. Melt the butter in a large frying pan. Add the onions and cook over a low heat for 25–30 minutes, stirring occasionally until very soft and well caramelized. Meanwhile, remove any tubes and membrane from the liver. Slice into more even-sized pieces and pat dry with absorbent kitchen paper. Flatten the unpeeled garlic cloves with the base of a pan.

2. Preheat the grill to high and grill the bacon for 3–4 minutes until crispy. Cut each rasher in half. Set aside.

3. Slide the onions onto a plate. Add 1½ tablespoons of the olive oil and the garlic cloves to the pan. Fry gently for 1–2 minutes until golden brown, then discard the garlic.

4. Turn up the heat and fry the liver with the sage leaves in the frying pan in batches for about 1 minute on each side, adding a little more oil if necessary. The liver should be browned on the outside and pink in the middle. Set aside with the bacon.

5. Slide the onions and their buttery juices back into the pan. Sprinkle with the flour and cook stirring for 1 minute. Stir in the stock and sherry, then bring to the boil and simmer for 2–3 minutes until thickened. Return the liver to the pan, stir together and season with salt and pepper. Top with the bacon and serve with mashed potatoes or soft polenta.

1
1
4

Gammon Steak with Fried Egg & Chips

PREP TIME: 15 minutes

COOKING TIME: 15–20 minutes

nutritional information per serving	752 kcals, 42g fat, 9g sat fat, 2g total sugars, 4.2g salt

Gammon steaks take only a few minutes to cook under a hot grill - just add a fried egg and home-made chips for a perfect pub-style dinner.

INGREDIENTS

- vegetable oil, for frying and brushing
- 6 large potatoes, such as Desirée or Maris Piper, cut into even-sized chips
- 4 gammon steaks, each about 175 g/6 oz
- 4 eggs
- salt and pepper

1. Heat enough oil for deep-frying in a large saucepan or deep-fryer to 120°C/250°F, checking the temperature with a thermometer, to blanch the chips. Preheat the oven to 150°C/300°F/Gas Mark 2.

2. Fry the chips for about 8–10 minutes, depending on size, until soft but not coloured. Remove from the oil, drain on kitchen paper and place in a warmed dish in the preheated oven. Increase the temperature of the oil to 180-190°C/350-375°F, or until a cube of bread browns in 30 seconds.

3. Meanwhile, place the gammon steaks on a grill pan and brush with a little oil. Preheat the grill to high and grill for 3–4 minutes on either side, turning occasionally until the fat is crisp. Set aside and keep warm.

4. Return the chips to the fryer at the increased temperature and cook for a further 2–3 minutes until they are golden brown and crisp. Drain, season well and keep warm.

5. Put 2 tablespoons of oil into a frying pan and heat over a medium heat. Break two eggs into the pan and cook for a few seconds until the white is setting. Tip the pan and spoon the hot oil over the egg yolks so that they become firm but still soft. Remove the eggs from the pan using a wooden spatula and drain on kitchen paper. Keep warm and repeat with the other eggs.

6. Arrange the gammon steaks, egg and chips on warmed plates and serve immediately.

2
3
5

Summer Roast Chicken

PREP TIME: 15 minutes plus resting

COOKING TIME: 1 hour 35 minutes

nutritional information per serving	424 kcals, 10g fat, 2g sat fat, 2g total sugars, 0.4g salt

Tempt them to the table with this aromatic roast chicken and new potatoes, flavoured with lemon and herbs.

INGREDIENTS

- 600 g/1 lb 5 oz new potatoes, scrubbed and larger ones halved
- 1 chicken, weighing 1.5 kg/3 lb 5 oz
- 1 lemon (preferably unwaxed)
- 1 tbsp chopped fresh thyme
- 2 tbsp olive oil
- 3 bay leaves
- 1 garlic bulb, cloves separated
- salt and pepper
- green salad, to serve

1. Parboil the potatoes in a pan of lightly salted boiling water for 10 minutes, then drain. Preheat the oven to 190°C/375°F/Gas Mark 5.

2. Loosen the skin over the chicken breast by pushing your fingers underneath, being careful not to tear it. Pare the zest from the lemon and mix it with the thyme, then push the mixture underneath the skin of the chicken. Drizzle in 2 teaspoons of the oil and season with salt and pepper. Cut the lemon in half and push the two pieces inside the body cavity with the bay leaves, then truss the chicken.

3. Transfer the potatoes to a large roasting tin. Add the garlic and remainder of the olive oil and toss together. Make a space for the chicken in the centre of the roasting tin and roast in the preheated oven for 1 hour 25 minutes, stirring and turning the potatoes once or twice during cooking. To check the chicken is cooked through, pierce the thickest part of the thigh with a skewer – when the juices run clear, it is ready. Cover and rest the chicken for 10–15 minutes before carving. Serve with the roast new potatoes and green salad.

1

2

3

COOK'S NOTE

If you would prefer the potatoes more crispy, turn the oven up to 200°C/400°F/ Gas Mark 6 and return them to the oven while the chicken is resting.

Puddings & Desserts

Sticky Toffee Pudding

SERVES 8

PREP TIME:
20 minutes

COOKING TIME:
35–40 minutes

nutritional information per serving	512 kcals, 19g fat, 11.5g sat fat, 67g total sugars, 0.8g salt

This is a divine pudding that anyone with a sweet tooth will love. The moist date and sultana sponge is smothered in a rich and creamy toffee sauce.

INGREDIENTS

- 75 g/2¾ oz sultanas
- 150 g/5½ oz dates, stoned and chopped
- 1 tsp bicarbonate of soda
- 25 g/1 oz butter, plus extra for greasing
- 200 g/7 oz soft light brown sugar
- 2 eggs
- 200 g/7 oz self-raising flour, sifted

sticky toffee sauce

- 25 g/1 oz butter
- 175 ml/6 fl oz double cream
- 200 g/7 oz soft light brown sugar

1. Preheat the oven to 180°C/350°F/Gas Mark 4. Grease a 20-cm/8-inch round cake tin.

2. To make the pudding, put the sultanas, dates and bicarbonate of soda into a heatproof bowl. Cover with boiling water and leave to soak. Put the butter into a separate bowl, add the sugar and mix well.

3. Beat the eggs into the butter mixture, then fold in the flour. Drain the soaked fruit, add to the bowl and mix. Spoon the mixture evenly into the prepared cake tin. Bake in the preheated oven for 35–40 minutes, or until a skewer inserted into the centre comes out clean.

4. About 5 minutes before the end of the cooking time, make the sauce. Melt the butter in a saucepan over a medium heat. Stir in the cream and sugar and bring to the boil, stirring constantly. Reduce the heat and simmer for 5 minutes. Cut the pudding into equal-sized portions, pour over the sauce and serve immediately.

2

2

3

BE PREPARED
The sponge can be made in advance. Reheat in a moderate oven or the microwave.

Chocolate Bread Pudding

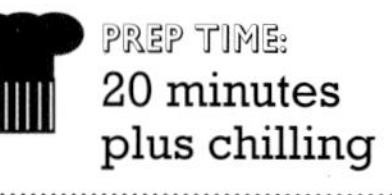

COOKING TIME: 35–40 minutes

nutritional information per serving	647 kcals, 33g fat, 19g sat fat, 41g total sugars, 1.7g salt

This comforting pudding is a great way to use up stale bread. It's flavoured with cocoa to give a lovely chocolate taste and served with smooth and sweet hot fudge sauce.

INGREDIENTS

- 6 slices thick white bread, crusts removed
- 450 ml/16 fl oz milk
- 175 ml/6 fl oz canned evaporated milk
- 2 tbsp cocoa powder
- 2 eggs
- 2 tbsp brown sugar
- 1 tsp vanilla extract
- icing sugar, for dusting

hot fudge sauce

- 55 g/2 oz plain chocolate, broken into pieces
- 1 tbsp cocoa powder
- 2 tbsp golden syrup
- 55 g/2 oz butter or margarine, plus extra for greasing
- 2 tbsp brown sugar
- 150 ml/5 fl oz milk
- 1 tbsp cornflour

1. Grease a shallow ovenproof baking dish. Cut the bread into squares and layer them in the dish.

2. Put the milk, evaporated milk and cocoa powder in a saucepan and heat gently, stirring occasionally, until the mixture is lukewarm. Whisk the eggs, sugar and vanilla extract together in a large jug. Add the warm milk mixture and beat well.

3. Pour into the prepared dish, making sure that all the bread is completely covered. Cover the dish with clingfilm and chill in the refrigerator for 1–2 hours, then bake in a preheated oven, 180°C/350°F/Gas Mark 4, for 35–40 minutes, until set. Leave to stand for 5 minutes.

4. To make the sauce, put all the ingredients into a saucepan and heat gently, stirring constantly until smooth.

5. Dust the chocolate bread pudding with icing sugar and serve immediately with the hot fudge sauce.

1
3
4

Rice Pudding with Poached Rhubarb

SERVES 4

PREP TIME: 20 minutes plus cooling

COOKING TIME: 1¼ hours

nutritional information per serving	412 kcals, 5.5g fat, 3.5g sat fat, 55g total sugars, 0.4g salt

Rose-scented chunks of sweet-sharp rhubarb complement the richness of this creamy pudding perfectly.

INGREDIENTS

- butter, for greasing
- 1.3 litres/2¼ pints whole or semi-skimmed milk
- 115 g/4 oz pudding rice
- 55 g/2 oz caster sugar
- 1 tsp vanilla extract
- freshly grated nutmeg, for sprinkling

poached rhubarb

- 400 g/14 oz rhubarb, cut into 5-cm/2-inch pieces
- 100 g/3½ oz caster sugar
- 3 tbsp water
- 1–2 tbsp rosewater or rose syrup

1. Preheat the oven to 160°C/325°F/Gas Mark 3. Grease a 1.4-litre/ 2½-pint baking dish or pie dish. Place the milk in a large, heavy-based saucepan and bring to the boil. Add the rice and boil for 10 minutes, stirring constantly at first so that it doesn't boil over.

2. Remove from the heat, stir in the sugar and vanilla extract. Transfer to the prepared dish and sprinkle with nutmeg. Bake in the preheated oven for 1¼ hours, or until a brown skin has formed on top and the pudding is still quite wobbly underneath.

3. Meanwhile, place the rhubarb in a baking dish or roasting tin just large enough to hold the pieces in a single layer. Add the sugar and water, and then stir the mixture.

4. Cover the tin tightly with foil and bake in the preheated oven for 30 minutes, or until the rhubarb is just tender when pierced with the point of a knife (very thick stems may need a little longer). Cool for at least 15 minutes, leaving the foil in place, then gently stir in the rosewater to taste. Spoon over the rice pudding and serve.

1

2

3

Queen of Puddings with Berry Fruits

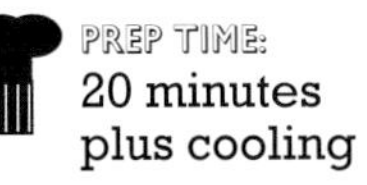

20 minutes plus cooling

COOKING TIME:
50–55 minutes

nutritional information per serving	366 kcals, 13.5g fat, 6.5g sat fat, 36g total sugars, 0.7g salt

A handful or two of fresh fruit complements the traditional jam filling in this dish perfectly.

INGREDIENTS

600 ml/1 pint milk
25 g/1 oz butter, plus extra for greasing
finely grated rind of 1 lemon
140 g/5 oz caster sugar
115 g/4 oz fresh white breadcrumbs
4 large eggs, separated
3 tbsp raspberry conserve or jam, warmed
125 g/4½ oz blueberries
125 g/4½ oz raspberries
single cream, to serve

1. Place the milk, butter and lemon rind in a saucepan. Heat to simmering point then add in 25 g/1 oz of the sugar and stir to dissolve. Remove from the heat and stir in the breadcrumbs. Leave to cool and soften the breadcrumbs for 20 minutes.

2. Preheat the oven to 160°C/325°F/Gas Mark 3. Whisk the egg yolks into the breadcrumb mixture and pour into a lightly greased 1.2-litre/2-pint baking dish. Bake in the preheated oven for 40 minutes or until just set in the middle. Leave the oven on.

3. Spread the conserve over the top of the pudding, being careful not to break the surface too much. Mix the blueberries and raspberries together and scatter over the top.

4. Place the egg whites in a clean bowl and whisk with an electric whisk until stiff peaks form. Slowly beat in the remaining sugar, one tablespoon at a time, until the meringue is thick and glossy. Spoon over the pudding, covering the top completely, and return to the oven for 10–15 minutes until just browned. Serve immediately with cream.

1

1

3

SOMETHING DIFFERENT

The fresh berries can be omitted or replaced with canned fruit.

Chocolate Pudding

SERVES 6

PREP TIME:
10 minutes

COOKING TIME:
10–15 minutes

nutritional information per serving	236 kcals, 13g fat, 8g sat fat, 19g total sugars, 1.3g salt

A rich and creamy chocolate dessert that tastes good, either warm or chilled.

INGREDIENTS

100 g/3½ oz sugar
4 tbsp cocoa powder
2 tbsp cornflour
pinch of salt
350 ml/12 fl oz milk
1 egg, beaten
55 g/2 oz butter
½ tsp vanilla extract
double cream, to serve

1. Put the sugar, cocoa powder, cornflour and salt into a heatproof bowl. Stir and set aside.

2. Pour the milk into a saucepan and heat over a medium heat until just simmering. Do not bring to the boil.

3. Keeping the pan over a medium heat, spoon a little of the simmering milk into the sugar mixture and blend, then stir this mixture into the milk in the pan. Beat in the egg and half of the butter and reduce the heat to low.

4. Simmer for 5–8 minutes, stirring frequently, until the mixture thickens. Remove from the heat and add the vanilla extract and the remaining butter, stirring until the butter melts and is absorbed.

5. The pudding can be served hot or chilled, with cream for pouring over. If chilling the pudding, spoon it into a serving bowl and leave to cool completely, then press clingfilm onto the surface to prevent a skin forming and chill in the refrigerator until required.

1

2

3

GOES WELL WITH

Lightly poach halved apricots in a little sugar and water and serve with the pudding.

Boozy Summer Pudding

SERVES 6

PREP TIME:
20 minutes
plus chilling

COOKING TIME:
3–4 minutes

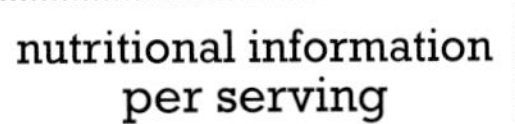

nutritional information per serving	196 kcals, 0.8g fat, 0.1g sat fat, 21g total sugars, 0.4g salt

An impressive pudding packed with juicy berries – there's almost no cooking involved so it's much easier to make than you might think.

INGREDIENTS

600 g/1 lb 5 oz mixed redcurrants, blackcurrants, blueberries and raspberries, plus extra to decorate (optional)

3–4 tbsp caster sugar

6 tbsp port

300 g/10½ oz strawberries, hulled and halved or quartered if large

6–7 slices thick white bread, crusts removed

double cream, to serve

1. Remove the currants from their stems and place in a saucepan with the rest of the fruit (except the strawberries), two tablespoons of the sugar and half the port. Simmer gently for 3–4 minutes until the fruit starts to release its juices. Remove from the heat. Add the strawberries and stir in the remaining sugar to taste.

2. Line a 1-litre/1¾-pint pudding basin with clingfilm, letting the ends overhang. Tip the fruit into a sieve set over a bowl to catch the juices, then stir the remaining port into the juices. Cut a circle the same size as the bottom of the basin out of one slice of bread. Dip in the juice mixture to coat and place in the bottom of the basin.

3. Reserve one slice of bread. Cut the rest in half slightly on an angle. Dip the pieces one at a time in the juice mixture and place around the sides of the basin, narrowest end down, pushing them together so there aren't any gaps and trimming the final piece of bread to fit (and any other pieces that are overhanging and need trimming).

4. Fill with the fruit then cover with the reserved piece of bread, cut to fit the top of the basin. Put a small plate on top and weigh it down with a can or two. Some juices may escape so place the basin on a plate to catch any spills. Chill overnight in the refrigerator. Set aside any remaining juice in the refrigerator.

5. Remove the weight and plate, then cover the pudding with a plate and flip over. Remove the bowl and clingfilm and decorate with extra summer fruits (if using). Serve with any remaining juice and cream.

1
3
4

Jam Roly-Poly

SERVES 6

PREP TIME:
25 minutes
plus resting

COOKING TIME:
1½–2 hours

nutritional information per serving	329 kcals, 18g fat, 9g sat fat, 10g total sugars, 0.5g salt

Bring back childhood memories of traditional school dinners with this classic suet and strawberry jam pudding.

INGREDIENTS

225 g/8 oz self-raising flour
pinch of salt
115 g/4 oz suet
grated rind of 1 lemon
1 tbsp sugar
50 ml/2 fl oz milk, plus 2 tbsp for brushing
50 ml/2 fl oz water
4–6 tbsp strawberry jam
ready-made custard, to serve

1. Sift the flour into a mixing bowl and add the salt and suet. Mix together well. Stir in the lemon rind and the sugar.

2. Mix together the milk and the water in a jug. Make a well in the centre of the dry ingredients and add the liquid ingredients to give a light, elastic dough. Knead lightly until smooth. If you have time, wrap the dough in clingfilm and leave it to rest for 30 minutes.

3. Roll the dough into a 20 x 25-cm/8 x 10-inch rectangle.

4. Spread the jam over the dough, leaving a 1-cm/½-inch border. Brush the border with the milk and roll up the dough carefully, like a Swiss roll, from one short end. Seal the ends. Wrap the roly-poly loosely in greaseproof paper and then in foil, sealing the ends well.

5. Prepare a steamer by half filling it with water and putting it on to boil. Place the roly-poly in the steamer and steam over rapidly boiling water for 1½–2 hours, making sure you top up the water from time to time.

6. When cooked, remove from the steamer and leave to cool slightly. Unwrap, cut into slices and serve immediately with the custard.

1
3
4

Lemon & Lime Posset

SERVES 4

PREP TIME:
10 minutes
plus chilling

COOKING TIME:
3 minutes

nutritional information per serving	771 kcals, 67g fat, 42g sat fat, 40g total sugars, trace salt

A dessert that tastes as if you've spent hours in the kitchen, even though it takes just minutes and is hardly any effort to prepare!

INGREDIENTS

- 500 ml/18 fl oz double cream
- 140 g/5 oz caster sugar
- finely grated rind and juice of 1 large lemon
- finely grated rind and juice of 1 lime, plus extra rind to serve
- 200 g/7 oz strawberries, hulled and halved
- shortbread biscuits, to serve

1. Place the cream and sugar in a saucepan. Bring slowly to the boil and simmer for 3 minutes, stirring occasionally.

2. Remove from the heat, add the lemon and lime rind and juices and whisk well. Pour into four glasses, leave to cool then cover and place in the refrigerator for about 2–3 hours until set and well chilled.

3. Divide the strawberries and extra lime rind between the glasses and serve with shortbread biscuits.

BE PREPARED

This recipe is ideal for entertaining as it can be made the day before. Add the strawberries just before serving.

Spotted Dick

 SERVES 6

PREP TIME: 15 minutes

COOKING TIME: 1–1½ hours

nutritional information per serving	409 kcals, 19.5g fat, 11g sat fat, 26g total sugars, 0.4g salt

This old-fashioned steamed suet pudding is 'spotted' with currants or raisins and flavoured with lemon.

INGREDIENTS

225 g/8 oz self-raising flour, plus extra for dusting
115 g/4 oz suet
55 g/2 oz caster sugar
140 g/5 oz currants or raisins
grated rind of 1 lemon
150–175 ml/5–6 fl oz milk
2 tsp melted butter, for greasing
ready-made custard, to serve

1. Mix together the flour, suet, sugar, currants and lemon rind in a mixing bowl.

2. Pour in the milk and stir together to give a fairly soft dough.

3. Turn out onto a floured surface and roll into a cylinder. Wrap in greaseproof paper that has been well-greased with the melted butter and seal the ends, allowing room for the pudding to rise. Overwrap with foil and place in a steamer over a saucepan of boiling water.

4. Steam for about 1–1½ hours, topping up the water level in the saucepan from time to time.

5. Remove the pudding from the steamer and unwrap. Place on a warmed plate and cut into thick slices. Serve with lots of custard.

1

3

3

SOMETHING DIFFERENT Replace the dried fruit with chopped mixed peel, if liked.

Yorkshire Curd Tart

SERVES 8

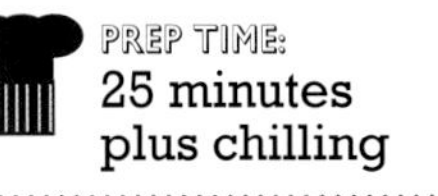

PREP TIME:
25 minutes
plus chilling

COOKING TIME:
1 hour

nutritional information per serving	285 kcals, 14g fat, 5g sat fat, 15g total sugars, 0.7g salt

A cross between a baked cheesecake and custard tart made with easy-to-find cottage cheese instead of the traditional fresh curds.

INGREDIENTS

- 300 g/10½ oz ready-made shortcrust pastry
- flour, for dusting
- 300 g/10½ oz cottage cheese
- 2 large eggs, lightly beaten
- 70 g/2½ oz caster sugar
- finely grated rind of 1 lemon
- 55 g/2 oz currants
- freshly grated nutmeg
- pouring cream, to serve (optional)

1. Roll out the pastry on a lightly floured surface. Use it to line a 20-cm/8-inch flan tin about 3 cm/1¼ inches deep. Prick the base and chill for 20 minutes.

2. Preheat the oven to 200°C/400°F/Gas Mark 6. Line the pastry case with baking paper and fill with baking beans. Bake blind in the preheated oven for 15 minutes, then remove the beans and paper and return to the oven for 5–10 minutes to crisp the base. Reduce the oven temperature to 180°C/350°F/Gas Mark 4.

3. Meanwhile, rub the cottage cheese through a sieve into a large bowl. Add the eggs, sugar and lemon rind to the cottage cheese and mix well, then stir in the currants. Pour the mixture into the pastry case and sprinkle a little nutmeg over the top. Bake in the preheated oven for 35 minutes until the filling is browned and just set in the middle.

4. Leave to cool, then remove from the tin. Serve with pouring cream (if using).

1

2

3

College Pudding

SERVES 6

PREP TIME:
15 minutes

COOKING TIME:
2½ hours

nutritional information per serving	416 kcals, 14g fat, 1g sat fat, 37g total sugars, 0.7g salt

A hearty steamed fruit pudding thought to have its origins in the student halls of Oxford and Cambridge.

INGREDIENTS

- butter, for greasing
- 100 g/3½ oz self-raising flour
- ½ tsp ground mixed spice (optional)
- pinch of salt
- 100 g/3½ oz fresh white breadcrumbs
- 100 g/3½ oz reduced-fat vegetable suet or shredded suet
- 100 g/3½ oz raisins
- 100 g/3½ oz currants
- 70 g/2½ oz soft dark brown sugar
- 25 g/1 oz chopped mixed peel
- 2 large eggs, lightly beaten
- 6–7 tbsp milk
- warmed golden syrup, to serve
- ready-made custard, to serve

1. Lightly grease an 850-ml/1½-pint pudding basin. Sift the flour, ground mixed spice (if using) and salt into a bowl. Add the breadcrumbs, suet, dried fruit, sugar and peel. Mix well.

2. Stir in the eggs and enough milk to make a soft dropping consistency. Spoon into the prepared basin and level the surface.

3. Cover the basin with baking paper and foil making a pleat in the centre to allow the pudding to rise, then secure with string. Steam the pudding in a covered saucepan half-filled with water for 2½ hours, topping the pan up with boiling water, if necessary. Turn out onto a warmed plate. Serve with golden syrup and custard.

1

2

2

SOMETHING DIFFERENT

If your family doesn't like mixed peel, replace with the finely grated rind of a lemon and an orange.

Lemon Meringue Pie

COOKING TIME:
55 minutes

nutritional information per serving	315 kcals, 13g fat, 7g sat fat, 27g total sugars, 0.3g salt

This much-loved English dessert is a real winner served warm or cold with cream. Choose plump lemons that feel heavy for their size to extract the most juice for the tangy filling.

INGREDIENTS

pastry

- 150 g/5½ oz plain flour, plus extra for dusting
- 85 g/3 oz butter, cut into small pieces, plus extra for greasing
- 35 g/1¼ oz icing sugar, sifted
- finely grated rind of ½ lemon
- ½ egg yolk, beaten
- 1½ tbsp milk

filling

- 3 tbsp cornflour
- 300 ml/10 fl oz water
- juice and grated rind of 2 lemons
- 175 g/6 oz caster sugar
- 2 eggs, separated

1. To make the pastry, sift the flour into a bowl. Rub in the butter with your fingertips until the mixture resembles fine breadcrumbs. Mix in the remaining pastry ingredients. Turn out onto a lightly floured work surface and knead briefly. Roll into a ball, wrap in clingfilm and chill in the refrigerator for 30 minutes.

2. Preheat the oven to 180°C/350°F/Gas Mark 4. Grease a 20-cm/8-inch round tart tin. Roll out the pastry to a thickness of 5 mm/¼ inch, then use it to line the base and side of the tin. Prick all over with a fork, line with baking paper and fill with baking beans. Bake blind in the preheated oven for 15 minutes. Remove the pastry case from the oven and take out the paper and beans. Reduce the oven temperature to 150°C/300°F/Gas Mark 2.

3. To make the filling, mix the cornflour with a little of the water to form a paste. Put the remaining water in a saucepan. Stir in the lemon juice, lemon rind and cornflour paste. Bring to the boil, stirring. Cook for 2 minutes. Leave to cool slightly. Stir in 5 tablespoons of the caster sugar and the egg yolks, then pour into the pastry case.

4. Whisk the egg whites in a clean bowl until stiff. Gradually whisk in the remaining caster sugar and spread the meringue over the pie. Bake for a further 40 minutes. Remove from the oven, cool and serve.

1
2
3

White Wine & Honey Syllabub

SERVES 4

PREP TIME:
15 minutes
plus chilling

COOKING TIME:
No cooking

nutritional information per serving	947 kcals, 88g fat, 51g sat fat, 25g total sugars, trace salt

This traditional English dessert made from whipped cream can be flavoured in many ways. Serve in small portions with delicate sponge fingers or brandy snaps.

INGREDIENTS

3 tbsp brandy
3 tbsp white wine
600 ml/1 pint double cream
6 tbsp clear honey
55 g/2 oz flaked almonds

1. Combine the brandy and wine in a bowl.

2. Pour the cream into a separate large bowl and whip until just thickened. Add the honey to the cream and whip for about 15 seconds.

3. Pour the brandy and wine mixture in a continuous stream into the cream and honey mixture, whipping constantly, until the mixture forms soft peaks.

4. Spoon into serving dishes. Transfer to the refrigerator and leave to chill for 2–3 hours. Scatter over the flaked almonds and serve.

SOMETHING DIFFERENT

Instead of brandy you could use sweet sherry or Madeira wine and add a little grated lemon zest too.

Syrup Sponge with Custard

SERVES 4

PREP TIME: 10 minutes

COOKING TIME: 10 minutes

nutritional information per serving	509 kcals, 29g fat, 17g sat fat, 33g total sugars, 1.3g salt

This warm sponge cake, flavoured with golden syrup and served with custard, brings back all the best memories of school dinner puddings.

INGREDIENTS

4 tbsp golden syrup

125 g/4½ oz butter, plus extra for greasing

85 g/3 oz caster sugar

2 eggs, lightly beaten

125 g/4½ oz self-raising flour

1 tsp baking powder

about 2 tbsp warm water

ready-made custard, to serve

1. Grease a 1.5-litre/2¾-pint pudding basin or microwave-safe bowl with butter. Spoon the golden syrup into the prepared basin.

2. Beat the butter with the sugar in a bowl until pale and fluffy. Gradually add the eggs, beating well after each addition.

3. Sift together the flour and baking powder, then gently fold into the butter mixture. Add enough water to give a soft, dropping consistency. Spoon the mixture into the basin and level the surface.

4. Cover with microwave-safe clingfilm, leaving a small space to let the air escape. Cook in a microwave oven on high for 4 minutes, then remove and leave the pudding to stand for 5 minutes while it continues to cook.

5. Turn the pudding out onto a serving plate. Serve immediately with custard.

1
2
4

Treacle Tart

SERVES 8

PREP TIME:
20 minutes
plus chilling

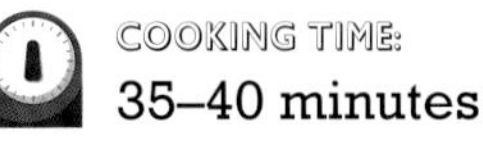

COOKING TIME:
35–40 minutes

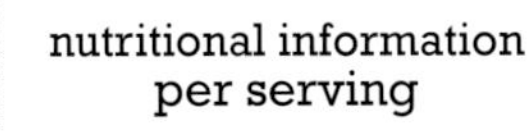

nutritional information per serving	404 kcals, 7.5g fat, 8g sat fat, 34g total sugars, 0.9g salt

Turn a few simple ingredients into this traditional warming winter pudding. Delicious served with thick cream.

INGREDIENTS

- 250 g/9 oz ready-made shortcrust pastry
- plain flour, for dusting
- 350 g/12 oz golden syrup
- 125 g/4½ oz fresh white breadcrumbs
- 125 ml/4 fl oz double cream
- finely grated rind of ½ lemon or orange
- 2 tbsp lemon juice or orange juice
- whipped cream or clotted cream, to serve

1. Roll out the pastry on a lightly floured work surface and use to line a 20-cm/8-inch tart tin, reserving the pastry trimmings. Prick the base of the pastry case all over with a fork, cover with clingfilm and chill in the refrigerator for 30 minutes. Re-roll the reserved pastry trimmings and cut out small shapes, such as leaves, stars or hearts, to decorate the top of the tart.

2. Preheat the oven to 190°C/375°F/Gas Mark 5. Mix the golden syrup, breadcrumbs, double cream and lemon rind with the lemon juice in a small bowl.

3. Pour the mixture into the pastry case and decorate the top of the tart with the pastry shapes of your choice. Transfer to the preheated oven and bake for 35–40 minutes, or until the filling is just set.

4. Leave the tart to cool slightly before serving. Cut into wedges and serve with cream.

1

2

3

COOK'S NOTE

Bake the tart on a preheated baking sheet to ensure the pastry base cooks properly.

Chocolate & Ale Ice Cream

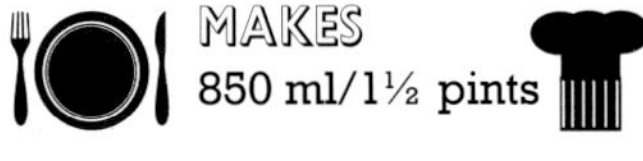

MAKES
850 ml/1½ pints

PREP TIME:
20 minutes plus chilling

COOKING TIME:
20–25 minutes

nutritional information per batch	3074 kcals, 199g fat, 115g sat fat, 265g total sugars, 0.8g salt

This extremely rich ice cream is a decadent treat - the dark ale flavour is subtle and perfectly matched by the bittersweet chocolate.

INGREDIENTS

350 ml/12 fl oz milk
150 g/5½ oz sugar
150 g/5½ oz plain chocolate (at least 85 per cent cocoa solids), broken into small pieces
4 egg yolks
1 tsp vanilla extract
325 ml/11 fl oz dark ale or stout
225 ml/8 fl oz double cream
grated chocolate, to decorate

1. Pour the milk into a saucepan and add the sugar. Bring to the boil, stirring, until the sugar has dissolved. Remove from the heat and stir in the chocolate.

2. Pour the egg yolks into a heatproof bowl and beat for 5 minutes, or until the whisk leaves a faint trail when lifted from the mixture. Stir some of the warm chocolate mixture into the egg yolks, then gradually beat in the rest.

3. Place the bowl over a pan of gently boiling water. Stir constantly for about 10 minutes, until the mixture reaches a temperature of 85°C/185°F, or is thick enough to coat the back of a spoon. Do not boil.

4. Strain the mixture through a fine strainer into a jug. Stir in the vanilla extract. Sit the base of the jug in iced water until cold, then cover with clingfilm and chill for 2 hours.

5. Meanwhile, pour the ale into a saucepan and bring to the boil. Reduce the heat and simmer briskly for 8 minutes, until reduced to 225 ml/8 fl oz. Pour into a jug, leave to cool, then chill.

6. Stir the cream and chilled ale into the chocolate mixture, mixing well. Pour the mixture into the bowl of an ice-cream machine. Churn and freeze according to the manufacturer's directions. Alternatively, pour the mixture into a shallow, freezerproof container, cover with clingfilm and freeze for about 2 hours, until beginning to harden around the edges. Beat until smooth to get rid of any ice crystals. Freeze again, repeat the process twice, then freeze until completely firm. Transfer to the refrigerator 30 minutes before serving to soften. Serve in chilled dishes, sprinkled with grated chocolate.

1
3
6

Sussex Pond Pudding

SERVES 6

PREP TIME:
20 minutes

COOKING TIME:
3½–4 hours

nutritional information per serving	535 kcals, 36g fat, 22g sat fat, 21g total sugars, 0.7g salt

This is a traditional steamed suet pudding originating from the southern county of Sussex.

INGREDIENTS

225 g/8 oz self-raising flour
125 g/4½ oz vegetable suet
75 ml/2½ fl oz milk
125 g/4½ oz unsalted butter, softened, plus extra for greasing
125 g/4½ oz soft light brown sugar
1 large unwaxed lemon
single cream, to serve

1. Lightly grease a 1.4-litre/2½-pint pudding basin. Mix the flour and suet together in a mixing bowl. Pour in the milk and mix to form a soft dough. Reserve one third of the dough to make a lid. Roll out the rest to a circle and press gently into the prepared basin.

2. Cream the butter and sugar together and place on the dough in the basin. Prick the lemon all over and stand it, pointed end down, on top of the butter and sugar mixture. Roll the remaining pastry into a circle and lay it over the top of the basin, pressing the edges down well to seal.

3. Cover the basin with baking paper and foil, making a pleat to allow the steam to rise. Tie with string around the rim. Fold some double thickness foil into a narrow strip to form a handle to lift the basin out of the pan. Steam the pudding in a covered pan half-filled with water, for 3½–4 hours, topping up with boiling water when needed. Remove the foil and parchment and loosen the pudding with a knife. Turn the pudding onto a warmed serving plate and serve with cream.

1

1

2

SOMETHING DIFFERENT

Add currants to the filling with the lemon to create a Kentish Puddle Pudding instead!

Hedgerow Fruit Crumble

PREP TIME:
20 minutes

COOKING TIME:
50–55 minutes

nutritional information per serving	393 kcals, 18g fat, 7g sat fat, 29g total sugars, 0.3g salt

Who can resist this easy and nostalgic pudding of crisp oaty crumble and sweet soft fruit?

INGREDIENTS

500 g/1 lb 2 oz cooking apples (two large ones), peeled and cut into bite-sized chunks

150 g/5½ oz blackberries

25 g/1 oz elderberries or blackcurrants

40 g/1½ oz demerara sugar

½ tsp ground cinnamon

1 tbsp water

crumble topping

175 g/6 oz plain flour

25 g/1 oz rolled oats

85 g/3 oz butter, diced

85 g/3 oz demerara sugar

55 g/2 oz hazelnuts, chopped

1. Preheat the oven to 190°C/375°F/Gas Mark 5. Place the apples, blackberries and elderberries in a 1.2-litre/2-pint baking dish. Stir in the sugar, cinnamon and water. Cover tightly with foil and bake in the preheated oven for 30 minutes until the apples are softened but not cooked right through.

2. For the crumble topping, mix the flour and oats together in a bowl. Add the butter and rub in with your fingertips until the mixture resembles fine breadcrumbs. Stir in the sugar and hazelnuts.

3. Remove the foil from the baked fruit and stir. Sprinkle the crumble mixture evenly over the top. Return to the oven for 20–25 minutes until lightly browned and starting to bubble at the edges. Serve immediately.

1

1

3

GOES WELL WITH

Try serving the crumble with vanilla or strawberry ice cream, Greek yogurt or even home-made brandy sauce (see page 314).

Oatmeal & Raspberry Pudding

SERVES 6

PREP TIME:
15 minutes
plus chilling

COOKING TIME:
5 minutes

nutritional information per serving	444 kcals, 37g fat, 22g sat fat, 9g total sugars, trace salt

This Scottish dessert is an irresistible concoction of raspberries and Scotch whisky-flavoured cream.

INGREDIENTS

90 g/3¼ oz rolled oats
350 ml/12 fl oz double cream
125 ml/4 fl oz single cream
3 tbsp whisky
2 tbsp honey, plus extra for drizzling
300 g/10½ oz fresh raspberries

1. Preheat the grill to medium. Spread out the oats on a baking sheet, place under the preheated grill and toast for 4–5 minutes, or until golden brown, stirring frequently to prevent burning. Transfer to a shallow bowl and leave to cool.

2. Combine the double cream, single cream, whisky and honey in a mixing bowl. Stir in the oats, mixing well. Cover with clingfilm and chill in the refrigerator for at least 2 hours or overnight to thicken. Stir occasionally to break up any clumps.

3. Set aside 40 g/1½ oz of the best raspberries to decorate. Lightly swirl the remaining raspberries into the oat mixture, creating pink streaks. Spoon into glass serving dishes, decorate with the reserved raspberries, drizzle with honey and serve immediately.

1
2
3

Sherry Trifle

SERVES 6

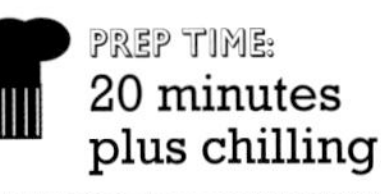
PREP TIME:
20 minutes plus chilling

COOKING TIME:
10 minutes

nutritional information per serving	518 kcals, 35g fat, 20g sat fat, 32g total sugars, 0.4g salt

Great for family celebrations, this retro classic is always popular. Forget jelly and stodgy blancmange though – this version has fresh strawberries and a rich and creamy vanilla custard.

INGREDIENTS

100 g/3½ oz trifle sponges
raspberry jam, for spreading
150 ml/5 fl oz sherry
150 g/5½ oz raspberries
350 g/12 oz strawberries, hulled and sliced

custard layer

6 egg yolks
50 g/1¾ oz caster sugar
500 ml/18 fl oz milk
1 tsp vanilla extract

topping

300 ml/10 fl oz double cream
1–2 tbsp caster sugar
1 chocolate bar, crumbled

1. Spread the trifle sponges with jam, cut them into bite-sized cubes and arrange in the bottom of a large glass serving bowl. Pour over the sherry and leave to stand for 30 minutes.

2. Combine the raspberries and strawberries and spoon them over the sponges in the bowl.

3. To make the custard, put the egg yolks and sugar into a bowl and whisk together. Pour the milk into a saucepan and warm gently over a low heat. Remove from the heat and gradually stir into the egg mixture, then return the mixture to the saucepan and stir constantly over a low heat until thickened. Do not boil. Remove from the heat, pour into a bowl and stir in the vanilla. Leave to cool for 1 hour. Spread the custard over the trifle, cover with clingfilm and chill in the refrigerator for 2 hours.

4. To make the topping, whip the cream in a bowl and stir in the sugar to taste. Spread the cream over the trifle, and then scatter over the chocolate pieces. Chill in the refrigerator for 30 minutes before serving.

1
2
4

Gooseberry Fool

SERVES 4

PREP TIME:
15 minutes
plus chilling

COOKING TIME:
10 minutes

nutritional information per serving	460 kcals, 34g fat, 21g sat fat, 36g total sugars, trace salt

It's thought that this quintessentially summer pudding gets its quirky name from the French 'fouler' meaning 'to crush'.

INGREDIENTS

300 g/10½ oz gooseberries, topped and tailed
4 tbsp caster sugar
finely grated zest of 1 lime
1 tbsp water
250 ml/9 fl oz double cream
125 ml/4 fl oz elderflower cordial
shortbread biscuits and lime rind, to serve

1. Place the gooseberries in a saucepan with the sugar, lime zest and water. Heat until simmering then cover and cook for 10 minutes until the fruit bursts.

2. Transfer to a bowl and crush the fruit against the side of the bowl with a fork. Leave to cool completely then chill for 20 minutes.

3. Whisk the cream and elderflower cordial together with an electric whisk until the mixture holds its shape, then fold in the gooseberries. Spoon into four small glasses. Serve chilled with shortbread biscuits and decorated with lime rind.

SOMETHING DIFFERENT

Red gooseberries are usually sweeter than green ones, so start by stewing them with half the sugar then taste and add a little more if necessary.

Eton Mess

PREP TIME:
20 minutes

COOKING TIME:
45–50 minutes

nutritional information per serving	485 kcals, 32g fat, 20g sat fat, 44g total sugars, 0.2g salt

Named after the English public school where it originated, this divine mix of fresh strawberries, crushed meringues and whipped cream really can look as messy as you like! Assemble the dessert just before serving so the meringues stay crisp.

INGREDIENTS

- 3 egg whites
- 175 g/6 oz caster sugar
- 700 g/1 lb 9 oz strawberries
- 2 tbsp icing sugar
- 2 tbsp crème de fraise (strawberry) liqueur (optional)
- 300 ml/10 fl oz double cream
- 150 ml/5 fl oz single cream

1. Preheat the oven to 150°C/300°F/Gas Mark 2. Whisk the egg whites in a clean bowl using an electric mixer until thick and in soft peaks. Add the sugar gradually, whisking well after each addition. The meringue mixture should be glossy and firm. Spoon the meringue onto a baking sheet lined with baking paper and spread into a rough 30-cm/12-inch round. Cook in the preheated oven for 45–50 minutes until the meringue is firm on the outside but still soft in the centre. Remove from the oven and allow to cool.

2. Check over the strawberries and hull them. Place a third of the strawberries (choose the larger ones) in a liquidizer and purée with the icing sugar. Pour the purée into a bowl, add the liqueur, if using, and the remaining strawberries and turn in the sauce until well mixed. Whip together the double and single cream until thick but still light and floppy.

3. Break the meringue into large pieces and place half in a large glass serving bowl. Spoon over half the fruit mixture and half the cream. Layer up the remaining ingredients and lightly fold the mixtures together so you have a streaky appearance. Serve immediately after mixing or the meringues will soften.

1
1
2

Chocolate & Banana Sundae

SERVES 4

PREP TIME:
10 minutes

COOKING TIME:
5–6 minutes

nutritional information per serving	800 kcals, 51g fat, 27g sat fat, 68g total sugars, 0.4g salt

This classic ice-cream sundae is just perfect for an afternoon treat on a hot summer day.

INGREDIENTS

chocolate sauce

55 g/2 oz plain chocolate

4 tbsp golden syrup

15 g/½ oz butter

1 tbsp brandy or dark rum (optional)

sundae

150 ml/5 fl oz double cream

4 bananas, peeled

8 scoops vanilla ice cream

75 g/2¾ oz chopped mixed nuts, toasted

40 g/1½ oz milk or plain chocolate, grated

4 fan wafers, to serve

1. To make the chocolate sauce, break the chocolate into small pieces and place in a heatproof bowl with the golden syrup and butter. Set over a saucepan of gently simmering water until melted, stirring until well combined. Remove the bowl from the heat and stir in the brandy, if using.

2. To make the sundae, whip the cream until just holding its shape and slice the bananas. Place a scoop of ice cream in the bottom of each of four tall sundae glasses. Top with slices of banana, some chocolate sauce, a spoonful of cream and a generous sprinkling of nuts.

3. Repeat the layers, finishing with a good dollop of cream, then sprinkle with the remaining nuts and the grated chocolate. Serve with fan wafers.

1

2

3

COOK'S NOTE

Make sure to choose a good quality ice cream that won't melt too quickly.

Knickerbocker Glory

SERVES 4

PREP TIME:
20 minutes

COOKING TIME:
2 minutes

nutritional information per serving	843 kcals, 59g fat, 35g sat fat, 62g total sugars, 0.4g salt

For a reduced fat version of this dish, use fruit sorbet instead of ice cream and yogurt instead of the whipped double cream.

INGREDIENTS

melba sauce

175 g/6 oz raspberries

1½ tbsp icing sugar, sifted

chocolate sauce

40 g/1½ oz plain chocolate, chopped

1 tbsp soft light brown sugar

100 ml/3½ fl oz milk

filling

450 g/1 lb prepared fresh fruit (e.g. sliced banana, seedless grapes, hulled and halved strawberries, pineapple chunks, chopped nectarines, raspberries)

700 ml/1¼ pints vanilla ice cream (9 small scoops)

topping

200 ml/7 fl oz double cream, softly whipped

15 g/½ oz chopped mixed nuts, lightly toasted

4 fan wafers

4 pitted fresh cherries or maraschino cherries

1. To make the Melba sauce, place the raspberries and icing sugar in a food processor and blend to a purée. Rub through a sieve and discard the pips.

2. To make the chocolate sauce, place all the ingredients in a small, heavy-based saucepan and heat gently until melted. Stir well and simmer for 2 minutes. Cool.

3. Assemble the Knickerbocker Glory just before serving. Spoon alternate layers of fruit, ice cream and Melba sauce into four tall sundae glasses, filling them almost to the top.

4. Top each glass with a spoonful of cream, then drizzle with the chocolate sauce and sprinkle nuts on top. Add a wafer to each glass and finish with a cherry. Serve immediately.

1
2
2

Sides & Accompaniments

Perfect Roast Potatoes

PREP TIME:
25 minutes

COOKING TIME:
1¼ hours

nutritional information per serving	156 kcals, 7g fat, 1g sat fat, 0.7g total sugars, trace salt

Crisp and golden with steaming hot fluffy white flesh, roast potatoes are the ideal accompaniment for a traditional roast dinner. Follow this simple recipe for perfect results every time.

INGREDIENTS

70 g/2½ oz goose or duck fat or 5 tbsp olive oil

coarse sea salt

1 kg/2 lb 4 oz even-sized floury potatoes, such as King Edward, Maris Piper or Desirée

8 fresh rosemary sprigs, to garnish

1. Preheat the oven to 230°C/450°F/Gas Mark 8. Put the fat in a large roasting tin, sprinkle generously with sea salt and place in the preheated oven.

2. Meanwhile, cook the potatoes in a large saucepan of boiling water for 8–10 minutes until par-boiled. Drain well and, if the potatoes are large, cut them in half. Return the potatoes to the empty saucepan and shake vigorously to roughen their outsides.

3. Arrange the potatoes in a single layer in the hot fat and roast for 45 minutes. If they look as if they are beginning to char around the edges, reduce the oven temperature to 200°C/400°F/Gas Mark 6. Turn the potatoes over and roast for a further 30 minutes until crisp. Serve garnished with rosemary sprigs.

2

2

3

SOMETHING DIFFERENT

Toss the par-boiled potatoes in a little English mustard powder to give an extra golden crust.

Sweet Potato Mash

SERVES 6

PREP TIME:
15 minutes

COOKING TIME:
10–15 minutes

nutritional information per serving	233 kcals, 9g fat, 5g sat fat, 12g total sugars, 0.3g salt

Sweet potatoes mashed until smooth with butter and cinnamon make a colourful side dish with a wonderful flavour. Pop under a hot grill for a few minutes to crisp up the top if liked.

INGREDIENTS

1 kg/2 lb 4 oz sweet potatoes, chopped
4 tbsp butter
2 tbsp maple syrup
¼ tsp cinnamon
salt and pepper
finely chopped parsley or snipped chives, to garnish

1. Bring a large saucepan of salted water to the boil. Add the sweet potatoes, cover the pan and boil for 10–15 minutes, or until the potatoes are very tender.

2. Drain the potatoes, then return them to the hot pan over a very low heat until any excess moisture evaporates. Use a potato masher to mash them in the pan. Add the butter and continue mashing until creamy.

3. Stir in the maple syrup and cinnamon, then season to taste. Garnish with parsley and serve immediately.

1

2

3

SOMETHING DIFFERENT

For a slightly different flavour, replace the cinnamon with grated nutmeg.

Colcannon

SERVES 4

PREP TIME:
15 minutes

COOKING TIME:
20–25 minutes

nutritional information per serving	103 kcals, 4.5g fat, 2.5g sat fat, 4g total sugars, 0.1g salt

This fluffy mash with leeks and cabbage is a classic vegetable dish that is often served on St Patrick's Day.

INGREDIENTS

225 g/8 oz green cabbage, shredded
5 tbsp milk
225 g/8 oz floury potatoes, such as King Edward, Maris Piper or Desirée, diced
1 large leek, chopped
pinch of freshly grated nutmeg
knob of butter
salt and pepper

1. Cook the shredded cabbage in a saucepan of boiling salted water for 7–10 minutes. Drain thoroughly and set aside.

2. Meanwhile, in a separate saucepan, bring the milk to the boil and add the potatoes and leek. Reduce the heat and simmer for 15–20 minutes, or until they are cooked through. Remove from the heat, stir in the freshly grated nutmeg and thoroughly mash the potatoes and leek together.

3. Add the drained cabbage to the mashed potato and leek mixture, season to taste and mix together well.

4. Spoon the mixture into a warmed serving dish, making a hollow in the centre with the back of a spoon. Place the butter on top and serve the colcannon at once, while it is still hot.

BE PREPARED

Make a day or two in advance then reheat in a moderate oven until it is piping hot.

Neeps & Tatties

SERVES 5

PREP TIME:
15 minutes

COOKING TIME:
20–25 minutes

nutritional information per serving	141 kcals, 9.5g fat, 6g sat fat, 4.5g total sugars, 0.2g salt

This dish is a rustic Scottish mix of mashed swede (neeps) and potatoes (tatties), traditionally served on Burns Night with haggis. This dish also makes a good accompaniment to roast meats, sausages, stews or casseroles.

INGREDIENTS

- 450 g/1 lb swedes, diced
- 250 g/9 oz floury potatoes, such as King Edward, Maris Piper or Desirée, diced
- 55 g/2 oz butter, plus extra to serve
- whole nutmeg, for grating
- salt and pepper
- fresh parsley sprigs, to garnish

1. Bring a large saucepan of lightly salted water to the boil. Add the swedes and potatoes and cook for 20 minutes until soft. Test with the point of a knife – if not cooked, return to the heat for a further 5 minutes. Drain well.

2. Return the swede and potatoes to the empty saucepan and heat for a few moments to ensure they are dry. Add the butter and mash with a potato masher until smooth.

3. Season well with salt and pepper and stir through. Grate nutmeg into the mash to taste and serve immediately, garnished with the parsley and with a knob of butter on top.

1 2 2

HEALTHY HINT

Instead of the butter, stir in a couple of spoonfuls of natural yogurt.

Bombay Potatoes

nutritional information per serving	320 kcals, 10g fat, 5g sat fat, 8g total sugars, 0.3g salt

Indian food is a British favourite and this spiced potato dish is a classic accompaniment to curry. It's also great served with naan bread and cooling cucumber yogurt.

INGREDIENTS

1 kg/2 lb 4 oz waxy whole potatoes, such as Charlotte or Jersey Royals
2 tbsp vegetable ghee
1 tsp panch poran spice mix
3 tsp ground turmeric
2 tbsp tomato purée
300 ml/10 fl oz plain yogurt
salt
chopped fresh coriander, to garnish

1. Preheat the oven to 180°C/350°F/Gas Mark 4. Put the whole potatoes into a large saucepan of salted cold water. Bring to the boil, then simmer for about 15 minutes, until the potatoes are just cooked, but not tender. Drain the potatoes and cut each one into four pieces.

2. Heat the ghee in a separate saucepan over a medium heat and add the panch poran, turmeric, tomato purée, yogurt and salt to taste. Bring to the boil and simmer, uncovered, for 5 minutes.

3. Add the potatoes to the pan, then cover and cook briefly. Transfer to an ovenproof casserole. Cook in the preheated oven for about 40 minutes, or until the potatoes are tender and the sauce has thickened a little. Sprinkle with the chopped coriander and serve immediately.

1

2

3

COOK'S NOTE
Ghee is a type of clarified butter - it has a high burning point, making it ideal for frying.

Cheese & Mustard Dumplings

SERVES 4

PREP TIME:
10 minutes

COOKING TIME:
15–20 minutes

nutritional information per serving	250 kcals, 15g fat, 9g sat fat, 0.5g total sugars, 0.5g salt

Great comfort food, add them to your favourite casserole or drop into soups to make filling meals.

INGREDIENTS

115 g/4 oz self-raising flour
55 g/2 oz suet
40 g/1½ oz Parmesan cheese, finely grated
1 tbsp chopped fresh parsley or chives
2 tsp coarse grain mustard
5–6 tbsp cold water
salt and pepper

1. Sift the flour into a bowl. Add the suet, Parmesan cheese and parsley. Season to taste and mix well.

2. Mix the mustard in a small bowl with 5 tablespoons of the water. Add to the dry ingredients then mix lightly to a soft dough adding a little extra water if necessary.

3. Divide the dough into 12 and roll into balls – they will triple in size. Drop the dumplings into your casserole or soup, cover and cook in the oven or on the hob for 15–20 minutes, until puffed up and fluffy in the middle. Alternatively for baked dumplings, place the dough balls on a baking sheet and bake at 200°C/400°F/Gas Mark 6 for 15 minutes. These don't puff up as much but they're nice and crunchy on the outside.

1

2

3

HEALTHY HINT

Vegetable suet is available for non-meat eaters. Look out for the reduced-fat version.

Sage & Onion Stuffing

SERVES 10 | PREP TIME: 15 minutes | COOKING TIME: 50 minutes

nutritional information per serving	127 kcals, 7g fat, 2.5g sat fat, 3.5g total sugars, 0.6g salt

A good stuffing is a must to serve with roast poultry – especially the Christmas turkey. It can either be baked separately, as here, or used to stuff the neck end of a bird before roasting.

INGREDIENTS

- 550 g/1 lb 4 oz pork sausage meat
- 1 onion, grated
- 350 g/12 oz cooking apple, cored and finely chopped
- 25 g/1 oz fresh white breadcrumbs
- 2 tbsp chopped fresh sage or marjoram
- grated rind of 1 lemon
- 1 egg, beaten
- sage sprig, to garnish

1. Preheat the oven to 200°C/400°F/Gas Mark 6. Place the sausage meat, onion, 300 g/10½ oz of the cooking apple, breadcrumbs, sage, lemon rind and egg in a large bowl and mix together until thoroughly combined.

2. Sprinkle the sausage mixture with the reserved chopped apple and then place in a 900 g/2 lb loaf tin or shape into balls and place on a baking sheet.

3. Bake in the preheated oven for 50 minutes, until the apple is golden and the sausage meat is cooked through. Garnish with a sprig of sage and serve immediately.

1

1

2

SOMETHING DIFFERENT

Replace the apple with finely chopped ready-to-eat dried apricots or cooked chestnuts.

Mini Yorkshire Puddings

 MAKES 6

PREP TIME: 15 minutes

 COOKING TIME: 30–35 minutes

nutritional information per pudding	178 kcals, 9g fat, 4g sat fat, 2g total sugars, 0.5g salt

Yorkshire pudding was traditionally made as a cheap dish to fill everyone up before the more expensive meat came to the table. Nowadays, it's always served alongside the roast beef! Try these chic mini versions for a special Sunday lunch.

INGREDIENTS

- 30 g/1 oz beef dripping or 2 tbsp sunflower oil
- 140 g/5 oz plain flour
- ½ tsp salt
- 2 eggs
- 225 ml/8 fl oz milk

1. Grease six metal pudding moulds with the dripping, then divide the remaining dripping between the moulds. Preheat the oven to 220°C/425°F/Gas Mark 7, placing the moulds in the oven so the dripping can melt while the oven heats.

2. Sift the flour and salt together into a large mixing bowl and make a well in the centre. Break the eggs into the well, add the milk and beat, gradually drawing in the flour from the side to make a smooth batter. Remove the moulds from the oven and spoon in the batter until they are about half full.

3. Bake in the preheated oven for 30–35 minutes, without opening the door, until the puddings are well risen, puffed and golden brown. Serve immediately, as they will collapse if left to stand.

1

2

2

FREEZING TIP

Yorkshires freeze really well - reheat from frozen in a hot oven for 8-10 minutes.

Braised Red Cabbage with Plums & Juniper

SERVES 4 | PREP TIME: 15 minutes | COOKING TIME: 50–55 minutes

nutritional information per serving	111 kcals, 6g fat, 3g sat fat, 12g total sugars, 0.2g salt

Slow cooked, lightly spiced red cabbage is the ideal accompaniment to rich meat dishes, such as pork, goose, game or even sausages.

INGREDIENTS

- 25 g/1 oz butter
- 1 large red onion, thinly sliced
- 450 g/1 lb red cabbage, outer leaves removed
- 5 tbsp vegetable stock
- ¼ tsp ground cinnamon
- 5 juniper berries, lightly crushed
- finely grated rind and juice of ½ orange
- 2 tsp soft brown sugar
- 300 g/10½ oz firm ripe plums, stoned and halved or quartered if large
- salt and pepper

1. Melt the butter in a saucepan. Add the onion, cover and cook gently for 5 minutes until softened. Meanwhile, quarter and core the cabbage and shred finely.

2. Add the cabbage to the pan with the stock, cinnamon, junipers, orange rind, orange juice and sugar. Mix well. Cover and cook over a low heat for 35 minutes.

3. Stir in the plums and season with salt and pepper. Cover and cook for a further 10–12 minutes until tender. Serve immediately.

1

1

3

SOMETHING DIFFERENT

Replace the plums with a peeled, cored and chopped cooking apple, adding it with the cabbage.

Brussels Sprouts with Buttered Chestnuts

 SERVES 4

PREP TIME: 10 minutes

COOKING TIME: 10–12 minutes

nutritional information per serving	239 kcals, 18g fat, 7g sat fat, 5g total sugars, 0.2g salt

The humble sprout is given the star treatment here – lightly fried with butter, nutmeg, chestnuts and flaked almonds.

INGREDIENTS

350 g/12 oz Brussels sprouts, trimmed

3 tbsp butter

100 g/3½ oz canned whole chestnuts

pinch of grated nutmeg

salt and pepper

50 g/1¾ oz flaked almonds, to garnish

1. Bring a large saucepan of salted water to the boil. Add the Brussels sprouts and cook for 5 minutes. Drain thoroughly.

2. Melt the butter in a large saucepan over a medium heat. Add the Brussels sprouts and cook, stirring, for 3 minutes, then add the chestnuts and nutmeg. Season to taste and stir well.

3. Cook for a further 2 minutes, stirring, then remove from the heat. Transfer to a warmed serving dish, garnish with almonds and serve immediately.

SOMETHING DIFFERENT

Top with diced and crispy fried bacon or Italian pancetta for extra flavour.

Luxury Cauliflower Cheese

PREP TIME:
25 minutes

20 minutes

nutritional information per serving	332 kcals, 20g fat, 12g sat fat, 9g total sugars, 0.8g salt

Wine, fresh herbs and punchy Parmesan have been added to this modern version of the classic dish.

INGREDIENTS

600 g/1 lb 5 oz cauliflower florets (1 medium cauliflower)
150 ml/5 fl oz dry white wine
1 bay leaf
450 ml/16 fl oz milk
25 g/1 oz butter, cut into pieces
25 g/1 oz plain flour
70 g/2½ oz mature Cheddar cheese, grated
40 g/1½ oz Parmesan cheese, grated
1 tsp English mustard
1 tbsp snipped fresh chives
1 tbsp chopped fresh parsley
salt

1. Cook the cauliflower in a large saucepan of lightly salted boiling water for 6–8 minutes until tender but still firm to the bite. Drain well. Preheat the oven to 200°C/400°F/Gas Mark 6. Alternatively, preheat the grill to high.

2. Place the wine and bay leaf in a saucepan. Boil rapidly until the wine is reduced by half. Add the milk, butter and flour and whisk with a hand whisk until the butter has melted. Continue whisking until the sauce boils and thickens. Simmer for 1 minute.

3. Remove from the heat. Mix the cheeses together and stir two thirds into the sauce until smooth, then stir in the mustard, chives and parsley. Remove the bay leaf from the sauce.

4. Spoon a little of the sauce over the base of a shallow baking dish. Tip the cauliflower into the dish and spread out in an even layer. Spoon the remaining sauce over the top and sprinkle with the rest of the cheese. Bake in the preheated oven for 20 minutes until lightly browned and bubbling. Alternatively brown under the grill. Serve hot.

1

3

4

BE PREPARED

This dish can be prepared ahead - cover and place in the refrigerator until ready to cook. Allow an extra 5-10 minutes of cooking time.

Bread Sauce

SERVES 12

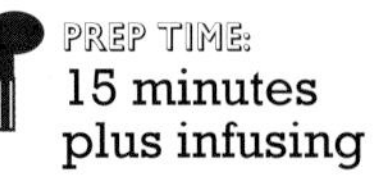

PREP TIME:
15 minutes
plus infusing

COOKING TIME:
20–25 minutes

nutritional information per serving	100 kcals, 5g fat, 3g sat fat, 3g total sugars, 0.3g salt

This simple but deliciously rich sauce is a classic accompaniment to roast turkey, but is also good with other roast meats and game.

INGREDIENTS

- 1 onion, peeled but left whole
- 12 cloves
- 1 bay leaf, plus extra to garnish
- 6 peppercorns
- 600 ml/1 pint milk
- 115 g/4 oz fresh white breadcrumbs
- 25 g/1 oz butter
- ½ tsp grated nutmeg, plus extra to garnish
- 2 tbsp double cream (optional)
- salt and pepper

1. Make 12 small holes in the onion using a skewer or sharp knife and stick a clove in each hole.

2. Place the onion, bay leaf and peppercorns in a small saucepan and pour in the milk. Place over a medium heat, bring to the boil, remove from the heat, then cover and leave to infuse for 1 hour.

3. Strain the milk and discard the onion, bay leaf and peppercorns.

4. Return the milk to the rinsed-out saucepan and add the breadcrumbs. Cook the sauce over a very gentle heat until the breadcrumbs have swollen and the sauce is thick. Stir in the butter and season well to taste.

5. When ready to serve, reheat the sauce briefly, if necessary. Add the nutmeg and stir in the double cream, if using. Pour into a warmed serving bowl and serve immediately, garnished with a bay leaf and nutmeg.

1

2

4

COOK'S NOTE

A food processor will make light work of making breadcrumbs, but don't over-process them.

Onion Gravy

SERVES 8

PREP TIME:
15 minutes

COOKING TIME:
1–1¼ hours

nutritional information per serving	91 kcals, 3.5g fat, 0.5g sat fat, 5.5g total sugars, 0.4g salt

The secret to well-flavoured gravy is to use a really good quality stock - home made if possible.

INGREDIENTS

2 tbsp sunflower oil
450 g/1 lb onions, thinly sliced
2 garlic cloves, crushed
1 tbsp sugar
25 g/1 oz plain flour
150 ml/5 fl oz red wine
600 ml/1 pint boiling beef or vegetable stock
2 tsp Dijon mustard
pinch of gravy browning (optional)
salt and pepper

1. Heat the oil in a large, heavy-based saucepan. Add the onions, garlic and sugar and fry over a low heat for 30 minutes, stirring occasionally, until very soft and light golden.

2. Stir in the flour and cook for 1 minute. Add the red wine and bring to the boil, then simmer and beat until the mixture is smooth. Add 150 ml/5 fl oz of the stock and return the mixture to the boil. Simmer and beat again to mix thoroughly.

3. Stir in the remaining stock, Dijon mustard and gravy browning, if using. Return the mixture to the boil once more and season to taste.

4. Simmer for 20 minutes and serve immediately.

1 1 3

SOMETHING DIFFERENT

Instead of the wine, you could add a splash of dry sherry, cider or port.

Tartare Sauce

SERVES 4

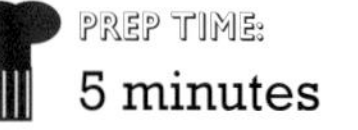

PREP TIME:
5 minutes

COOKING TIME:
No cooking

nutritional information per serving	63 kcals, 6g fat, 0.6g sat fat, 1.5g total sugars, 0.7g salt

A reduced-calorie and reduced-fat version of this popular sauce you can spoon on without feeling guilty - and it's just as delicious as the original!

INGREDIENTS

75 ml/2½ fl oz reduced-fat mayonnaise
75 ml/2½ fl oz fat-free fromage frais
1 tbsp finely chopped capers
1 tbsp finely chopped gherkin
1 tbsp chopped fresh parsley
½ lemon

1. Place the mayonnaise and fromage frais in a small bowl and mix together thoroughly.

2. Slowly mix in the chopped capers, chopped gherkin and chopped parsley. Stir to ensure everything is evenly distributed.

3. Squeeze roughly 1 tablespoon of lemon juice (or to taste) into the mixture and stir. Transfer to a small serving dish and serve immediately.

1

3

3

GOES WELL WITH

This sauce is often served with fish fried in breadcrumbs and fish cakes, but it is delicious with any plain grilled or fried fish dish.

Cranberry Sauce

SERVES 8

PREP TIME:
15 minutes

COOKING TIME:
15–20 minutes

nutritional information per serving	90 kcals, 0g fat, 0g sat fat, 19g total sugars, trace salt

This rich red sauce with its sweet and sharp flavour is as much part of a traditional Christmas lunch as turkey and stuffing!

INGREDIENTS

- thinly pared rind and juice of 1 lemon
- thinly pared rind and juice of 1 orange
- 350 g/12 oz cranberries, thawed if frozen
- 140 g/5 oz caster sugar
- 2 tbsp arrowroot, mixed with 3 tbsp cold water

1. Cut the strips of lemon and orange rind into thin shreds and place in a heavy-based saucepan. If using fresh cranberries, rinse well and remove any stalks. Add the berries, citrus juice and sugar to the saucepan and cook over a medium heat, stirring occasionally, for 5 minutes, or until the berries begin to burst.

2. Strain the juice into a clean saucepan and reserve the cranberries. Stir the arrowroot mixture into the juice, then bring to the boil, stirring constantly, until the sauce is smooth and thickened. Remove from the heat and stir in the reserved cranberries.

3. Transfer the cranberry sauce to a bowl and leave to cool. Cover with clingfilm and chill in the refrigerator until ready to serve.

FREEZING TIP
This sauce will freeze for up to two months. Thaw overnight in the refrigerator.

Rosemary-infused Mint Sauce

SERVES 6

PREP TIME:
10 minutes
plus cooling

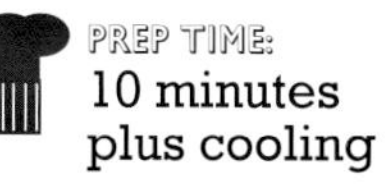
COOKING TIME:
No cooking

nutritional information per serving	13 kcals, 0.1g fat, 0g sat fat, 2.5g total sugars, 0.35g salt

Mint is one of the easiest herbs to grow. It's well worth it, just so you can make plenty of this fresh-tasting sauce whenever you fancy roast lamb!

INGREDIENTS

15 g/½ oz mint leaves
1 tbsp caster sugar
2 tsp very finely chopped fresh rosemary
generous pinch of sea salt
4 tbsp boiling water
4 tbsp white wine vinegar

1. Wash the mint leaves in a sieve and shake dry. Chop finely.

2. Place the mint in a bowl with the sugar, rosemary and salt. Pour over the boiling water and stir to dissolve the sugar. Leave for 20 minutes to cool.

3. Stir in the vinegar. Add a little more water or vinegar to taste if needed. Transfer to a small serving dish and serve immediately.

SOMETHING DIFFERENT

For a spicy mint sauce that's great with barbecued meats, add a deseeded, finely chopped green chilli.

Garlic & Chilli Piccalilli

MAKES
1.6 kg/
3 lb 8 oz

PREP TIME:
25 minutes
plus standing

COOKING TIME:
15–20 minutes

nutritional information per 100g	58 kcals, 0.8g fat, 0.1g sat fat, 8.5g total sugars, 0.9g salt

This sweet tangy mustard pickle is a useful way of using up surplus home-grown vegetables.

INGREDIENTS

- 350 g/12 oz cauliflower, broken into small florets
- 350 g/12 oz pickling onions or small shallots, halved
- 225 g/8 oz runner beans, de-stringed and cut into 2-cm/¾-inch pieces
- 225 g/8 oz courgettes or marrow, cut into 2-cm/¾-inch chunks
- 225 g/8 oz salt
- 1.7 litres/3 pints cold water (approximately)
- 150 g/5½ oz golden caster sugar
- 850 ml/1½ pints distilled malt vinegar
- 4 cm/1¾ inch piece of ginger, grated
- 5 garlic cloves, finely chopped
- 1 large mild red chilli, deseeded and finely chopped
- 1½ tbsp mustard seeds
- 1½ tbsp coriander seeds
- 4 tbsp cornflour
- 4 tsp ground turmeric
- 1 tbsp dry English mustard powder

1. Mix together the vegetables, salt and water in a large bowl. Cover and leave for 24 hours.

2. The next day, drain the vegetables, rinse well and drain again. Place them in a large saucepan with the sugar, 700 ml/1¼ pints of the vinegar, the ginger, garlic, chilli, mustard seeds and coriander seeds and bring to the boil. Simmer for 10–12 minutes until the vegetables are tender but still firm to the bite.

3. Blend the remaining vinegar with the cornflour, turmeric and mustard powder, then stir into the vegetables and simmer for 2–3 minutes until thickened. Transfer to hot sterilized jars, wipe the rims then seal the lids. You can eat the piccalilli straight away or store in a cool dark place for 1 to 2 months. Refrigerate once opened.

1
2
3

Corn Pickle

MAKES 600 g/ 1 lb 5 oz

PREP TIME: 15 minutes

COOKING TIME: 20–25 minutes

nutritional information per 100g	100 kcals, 1.5g fat, 0.2g sat fat, 4g total sugars, trace salt

A great way to use up a glut of fresh corn cobs in late summer, this tasty pickle goes particularly well with barbecued sausages and burgers.

INGREDIENTS

- 5 corn cobs, about 900 g/ 2 lb, husked
- 1 red pepper, deseeded and finely diced
- 2 celery sticks, very finely chopped
- 1 red onion, finely chopped
- 125 g/4½ oz sugar
- 2 tbsp mustard powder
- ½ tsp celery seeds
- small pinch of turmeric (optional)
- 225 ml/8 fl oz cider vinegar
- 125 ml/4 fl oz water
- salt

1. Bring a large saucepan of lightly salted water to the boil and fill a bowl with iced water. Add the corn to the boiling water, return the water to the boil and boil for 2 minutes, or until the kernels are tender-crisp. Using tongs, immediately plunge the cobs into the cold water to halt cooking. Remove from the water and cut the kernels from the cobs, then set aside.

2. Add the red pepper, celery and onion to the pan of corn cooking water, bring back to the boil and boil for 2 minutes, until tender. Drain well and return to the pan with the corn. Put the sugar, 1 tablespoon of salt, mustard, celery seeds and turmeric, if using, into a bowl and mix together, then stir in the vinegar and water. Add to the pan, bring to the boil, then reduce the heat and simmer for 15 minutes, stirring.

3. Ladle the relish into hot sterilized jars, filling them to within 1 cm/ ½ inch of the top of each jar. Wipe the rims then seal the lids. Leave to cool completely, then serve or refrigerate for up to 2 months.

1

2

2

COOK'S NOTE

To sterilize jars, wash thoroughly and place in a warm oven for 10-15 minutes.

Bread & Butter Pickle

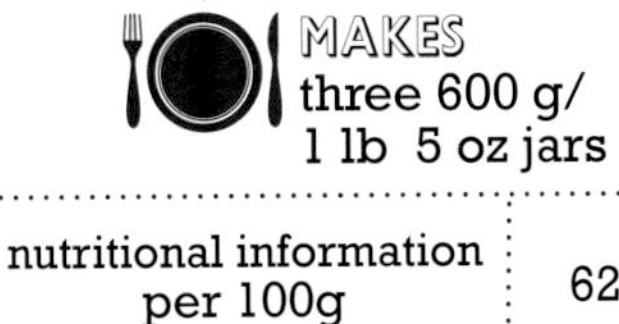

MAKES
three 600 g/
1 lb 5 oz jars

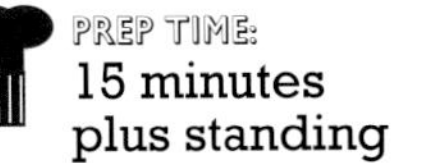

PREP TIME:
15 minutes
plus standing

COOKING TIME:
10–15 minutes

nutritional information per 100g	62 kcals, 0g fat, 0g sat fat, 13g total sugars, 1.9g salt

This delicious cucumber pickle is thought to have got its name because – like bread and butter – it was on everyone's table!

INGREDIENTS

3 cucumbers (about 1 kg/ 2 lb 4 oz), sliced
2 large onions, thinly sliced
40 g/1½ oz salt
600 ml/1 pint cracked ice
500 ml/18 fl oz cider vinegar
250 g/9 oz granulated sugar
2 tsp mustard seeds
½ tsp ground turmeric
½ tsp celery seeds

1. Place the cucumbers, onions, salt and ice in a large bowl. Mix well. Place a plate on top of the mixture and weigh it down with ice blocks. Leave to stand for 3 hours then drain well. Do not rinse.

2. Place the vinegar, sugar, mustard seeds, turmeric and celery seeds in a large saucepan. Heat the mixture until the sugar has dissolved, stirring constantly. Bring to the boil.

3. Add the cucumber and onions, then heat again until just boiling. Remove from the heat and transfer the vegetables to hot sterilized jars with a slotted spoon, leaving about 4 cm/1½ inches of room at the top.

4. Top up with the spiced vinegar liquid left in the pan, cover with vinegar-proof lids and seal. Store in the refrigerator once cooled. The vegetables start to taste pickled after a couple of hours and will keep in the refrigerator for about 3 weeks.

1 1 2

HEALTHY HINT

Don't be alarmed by the amount of salt. Most of it drains away with the melted ice and juices from the vegetables - the pickle doesn't taste salty at all.

Orange & Squash Marmalade

MAKES
2.25 kg/5 lb

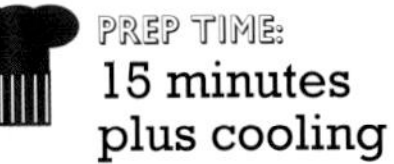
PREP TIME:
15 minutes
plus cooling

COOKING TIME:
1¼–1½ hours

nutritional information per 100g	190 kcals, 0g fat, 0g sat fat, 48g total sugars, trace salt

This modern savoury marmalade is flavoured with hot chillies and spicy fresh ginger. Serve with a cold meat platter or a mixed cheese board. Alternatively, try spreading a little over roast gammon or grilled pork chops to give a tangy glaze.

INGREDIENTS

900 g/2 lb acorn squash or butternut squash (peeled and deseeded weight), cut into small chunks

6 blood oranges, scrubbed

150 ml/5 fl oz freshly squeezed lemon juice

small piece fresh ginger, grated

2 serrano chillies, deseeded and finely sliced

1.2 litres/2 pints water

1.25 kg/2 lb 12 oz preserving sugar

1. Place the squash in a large saucepan with a tight-fitting lid. Thinly slice two of the oranges without peeling, reserving the pips, and add to the saucepan.

2. Peel the remaining oranges, chop the flesh and add to the pan together with the lemon juice, grated ginger and sliced chillies. Tie up the orange pips in a piece of muslin and add to the pan with the water.

3. Bring to the boil, then reduce the heat, cover and simmer gently for 1 hour, or until the squash and oranges are very soft. If preferred, transfer the mixture to a preserving pan.

4. Add the sugar and heat gently, stirring, until the sugar has completely dissolved. Bring to the boil and boil rapidly for 15 minutes, or until the setting point is reached.

5. Skim, if necessary, then leave to cool for 10 minutes. Remove the muslin bag. Pour into hot sterilized jars and immediately cover the tops with waxed discs. When completely cold, cover with cellophane or lids and store in a cool place. Refrigerate once opened.

1
1
2

Traditional Lemon Curd

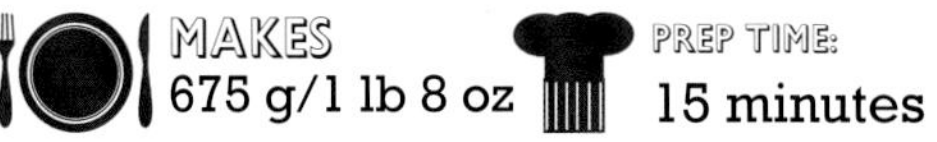

MAKES
675 g/1 lb 8 oz

PREP TIME:
15 minutes

COOKING TIME:
20–25 minutes

nutritional information per 100g	427 kcals, 17g fat, 10g sat fat, 65g total sugars, 0.4g salt

Home-made lemon curd has a sublime flavour with a velvety smooth texture. Time and patience is needed when cooking the mixture as it can curdle if cooked quickly over too high a heat.

INGREDIENTS

4 lemons (preferably unwaxed and organic), scrubbed and dried
4 eggs, beaten
115 g/4 oz unsalted butter, diced
450 g/1 lb sugar

1. Finely grate the rind from the lemons and squeeze out all the juice. Place the rind and juice in a heatproof bowl, stir in the eggs, then add the butter and sugar.

2. Place the bowl over a saucepan of gently simmering water, ensuring that the base of the bowl does not touch the water. Cook, stirring constantly, until the sugar has completely dissolved, then continue to cook, stirring frequently, until the mixture thickens and coats the back of the spoon.

3. Spoon into hot sterilized jars and immediately cover the tops with waxed discs. When completely cold, cover with lids and store in a cool, dark place. Refrigerate once opened.

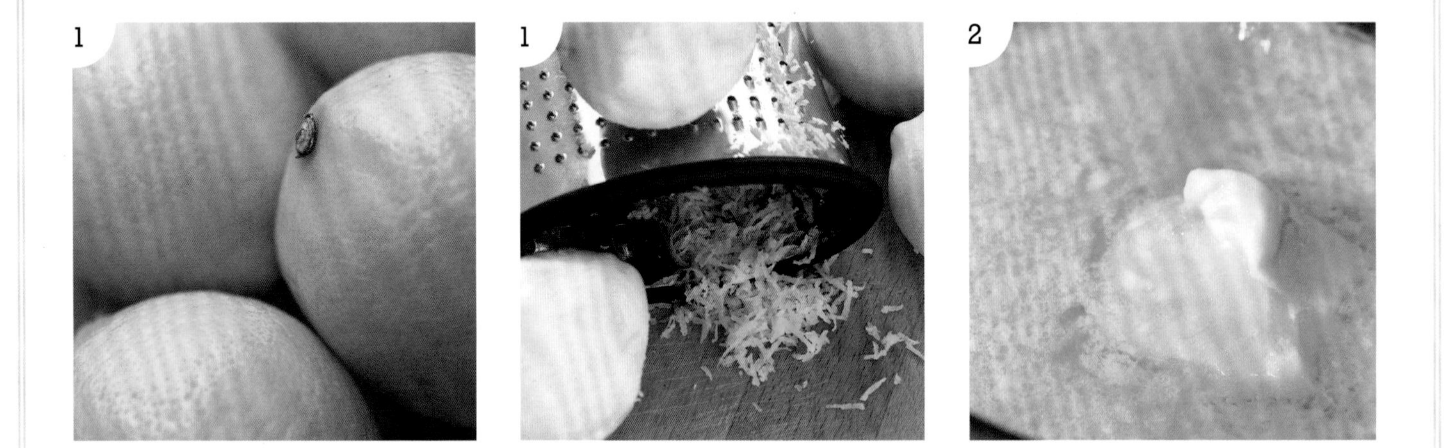

SOMETHING DIFFERENT

Replace one of the lemons with the juice and rind of two limes, if liked.

Classic Strawberry Jam

MAKES
1.5 kg/
3 lb 5 oz

PREP TIME:
10 minutes
plus cooling

COOKING TIME:
40–45 minutes

nutritional information per 100g	428 kcals, 1g fat, 0.5g sat fat, 106g total sugars, trace salt

Choose the freshest English summer strawberries to give your jam the best flavour. Take the family on a trip to a pick-your-own farm to buy a glut of strawberries - as well as being good value, you'll be able to ensure you have the finest specimens!

INGREDIENTS

1.5 kg/3 lb 5 oz ripe, unblemished whole strawberries, hulled and rinsed
juice of 2 lemons
1.5 kg/3 lb 5 oz preserving sugar
1 tsp butter

1. Place the strawberries in a preserving pan with the lemon juice, then simmer over a gentle heat for 15–20 minutes, stirring occasionally, until the fruit has collapsed and is very soft.

2. Add the sugar and heat, stirring occasionally, until the sugar has completely dissolved. Add the butter, then bring to the boil and boil rapidly for 15–20 minutes, or until the jam has reached its setting point.

3. Leave to cool for 8–10 minutes, then skim and pour into hot sterilized jars and immediately cover the tops with waxed discs. When completely cold, cover with cellophane or lids and store in a cool place. Refrigerate once opened.

1

1

2

COOK'S NOTE
Stir the jam before potting to prevent the berries from sinking to the bottom of the jars.

Home-made Vanilla Custard

SERVES 4

PREP TIME:
15 minutes
plus infusing

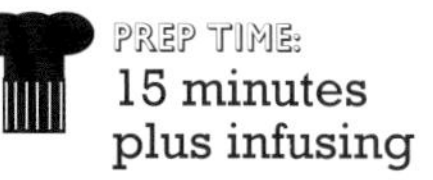

COOKING TIME:
15–20 minutes

nutritional information per serving	105 kcals, 6g fat, 3g sat fat, 6g total sugars, 0.15g salt

Smooth and creamy with a wonderful vanilla fragrance, this divine sauce is perfect for serving with hot or cold puddings or as a base for home-made vanilla ice cream.

INGREDIENTS

300 ml/10 fl oz milk
2 eggs
2 tsp caster sugar
1 vanilla pod, split
1 tsp vanilla extract (optional)

1. Put 2 tablespoons of the milk, the eggs and sugar into a heatproof bowl that will fit over a saucepan of simmering water without the bottom of the bowl touching the water, then set aside.

2. Put the remaining milk into a small, heavy-based saucepan over a medium-high heat and heat just until small bubbles appear around the edge. Scrape half the vanilla seeds into the milk and add the pod. Remove the pan from the heat, cover and leave to infuse for 30 minutes.

3. Bring a kettle of water to the boil. Meanwhile, using an electric mixer, beat the milk, eggs and sugar until pale and thick. Slowly beat in the warm milk.

4. Pour a thin layer of boiling water into a saucepan, place over a low heat and fit the bowl containing the milk mixture snugly on top. Cook, stirring constantly, for 10–15 minutes, until the sauce becomes thick enough to hold the impression of your finger if you rub it along the back of the spoon. It is important that the bottom of the bowl never touches the water and that the sauce doesn't boil. If the sauce looks as if it is about to boil, remove the bowl from the pan and continue stirring.

5. Strain the hot custard into a separate bowl and stir in the vanilla extract, if using. The custard can be used immediately, or left to cool completely, then covered and chilled for up to one day. The sauce will thicken on cooling.

1
3
5

Brandy Sauce

 SERVES 4

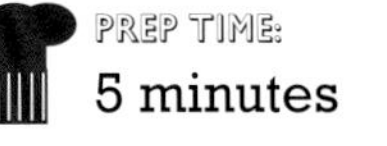 PREP TIME: 5 minutes

COOKING TIME: 5 minutes

nutritional information per serving	285 kcals, 24g fat, 15g sat fat, 3g total sugars, 0.1g salt

This sweet sauce is traditionally served at Christmas, but it goes down a treat served with fruit pies and sponge puddings at any time of the year.

INGREDIENTS

- 225 ml/8 fl oz milk
- 15 g/½ oz plain flour
- 15 g/½ oz butter, cut into small pieces
- 140 ml/4¾ fl oz double cream
- 4–5 tbsp brandy

1. Place the milk, flour and butter in a small saucepan. Heat gently, whisking constantly with a balloon whisk or hand whisk until the butter has melted.

2. Continue whisking until the sauce boils and thickens. Simmer gently for 1 minute.

3. Stir in the cream, and then stir in the brandy to taste. Heat through without re-boiling. Serve immediately.

SOMETHING DIFFERENT

Replace the brandy with rum and grate in a little nutmeg, or flavour with 2-3 tablespoons of orange liqueur.

Index